First-Rate Reading™

Literature-Based Activities that Support Research-Based Instruction

by 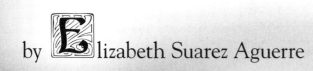lizabeth Suarez Aguerre

Grade K

Carson-Dellosa Publishing Company, Inc.
Greensboro, North Carolina

Credits
to *First-Rate Reading*™

Project Coordinator: Kelly Gunzenhauser

Editors: Ellen Holmes and Donna Walkush

Layout Designer: Jon Nawrocik

Cover Designer: Annette Hollister-Papp

Cover Illustrator: Bill Neville

Illustrators: Bill Neville and Wayne Miller

Dedication
of *First-Rate Reading*™

This book is dedicated to Pablo…

Thanks for cooking every meal, washing every dish, folding every shirt, and even doing the litter box…

I certainly could not have done this without you!

ISBN 0-88724-249-9

Table of Contents
to *First-Rate Reading*™

• *What is Put Reading First?*
By now, most educators are familiar with the Put Reading First federal initiative. Part of the No Child Left Behind Act, Reading First is the culmination of research designed to identify best practices for reading teachers. Reading First holds teachers accountable for students' mastery of five very specific components of literacy: phonemic awareness, phonics, fluency, vocabulary, and comprehension. Practices that focus on these components are already in use by many teachers, and several states have received grants to implement Reading First programs.

• *How will the* First-Rate Reading™ *series help me teach reading?*
In addition to the fact that literacy is a basic and necessary skill, the love of books and the desire to share that love inspires many teachers. Even in the face of increased standardized testing and skill-based instruction, fine children's literature continues to be an important part of reading curriculums. This series helps teachers connect great literature with lessons that reinforce the components of Reading First by:
  • providing additional phonemic awareness and phonics practice for students who need it
  • reinforcing phonics concepts with activities that conform to an existing, sequential phonics program
  • making teaching vocabulary strategies fun and relevant
  • creating opportunities for students to practice fluency skills with age-appropriate texts
  • engaging students in discussions and activities that help them comprehend what they read and apply those meanings to other literature and to their own lives

• *Why were these children's books chosen for this series?*
Teaching reading is much easier when students (and teachers) have a desire to read. These books were chosen because students respond to real, excellent literature (many are Caldecott Medal and Newbery Medal winners), and because they are student and teacher favorites. Attention is paid to old favorites, such as *Green Eggs and Ham* and *Frog and Toad Together*, as well as modern classics like *If You Take a Mouse to School* and *Because of Winn-Dixie*. There is truly something for every reader to enjoy.

• *Some activities and reproducibles seem very advanced/very easy for my class. How do I adjust them to fit different levels?*
After completing beginning-of-the-year assessments, you should have an idea of students' reading and writing skills. What may take longer to assess is their different abilities to work independently. At the kindergarten level, you should direct the activities by doing them in whole-class, small-group, or partner settings. Additionally, make the reproducibles more accessible by modeling what students should do, reading all words and directions aloud to them, saying the names of pictures and the sounds of letters, etc. For activities which require students to write, consider having students dictate their answers, since many young children cannot write more than a few letters or short words. Also, consider having students color every page on which there is art, both to give them fine-motor-skill practice and to let them make even dictated work "their own."

- *How do I actually use the children's books with the activities?*

Some activities use the actual text from the books, while others use themes that are similar to those in the books. For example, a phonics activity based around *Goodnight Moon* looks at the sounds the letter g makes, with Goodnight as the example. Other activities for *Goodnight Moon* use the art for work on positional words, and the text for retelling and comprehension questions. Page numbers in each children's book are referenced, but bear in mind that some books do not have page numbers, and that the numbering may change according to which edition you use.

- *How do I match these activities to the phonics system I have to follow, and how do I know when to choose which lesson?*

In the Table of Contents, all of the activities are listed by type. Some of the activities are general in what they teach (making predictions, alphabet practice, etc.) but are unique in how they are executed. Other activities are very specific in what they teach (/g/ sounds, ot word family, etc.). Since most beginning reading programs are driven by the order in which phonemic awareness and phonics elements are taught, it may be most convenient to refer to the Phonemic Awareness and Phonics key below, and base literature choices on how your program's phonics lessons correspond to the phonics key below.

Phonemic Awareness/Phonics
Key Page References

short /a/–58
/b/–8, 10, 30
short /e/–48
long /e/ (e, ea, ee)–8, 10, 18, 48
silent e–80
/g/ (hard and soft)–38, 40
/h/–98, 100
short /i/–58, 148
long /i/–128, 148
/l/–78
silent l–78
/m/–58
/n/–98, 100, 110
long /o/ (oa, o_e, ow)–130
/o/ diphthongs–28, 30
/o/ exceptions–138
/oo/–60
r-controlled vowels–28
/s/–118, 120
/t/–68
/w/–148, 150
/wh/–148
x (/ks/)–148
/y/–130, 138

alliteration–60
alphabet–18, 20, 88, 90, 130
consonant blends–48
consonant digraphs–150
initial letters–70, 90, 100, 110, 140
initial phonemes–38, 88, 108, 138, 140
blending or counting phonemes–98, 108
letter/sound correspondence–80
letter/word recognition–40
letters in words–80
long vowels–108
missing letters–110
onsets and rimes–70, 120
phoneme recognition–28, 128
phonics clues–140
rhymes (words, word families, phonemes)–18, 48, 68, 88, 118, 120, 128, 150
sound spelling–10, 50, 90, 100, 128
sounding out words–60, 110
spelling with manipulatives–10, 50, 70, 100
syllable work–8, 28, 38
tactile letter writing–20

Pronunciation Guide

to *First-Rate Reading*™

This book uses very simple descriptions of sounds in order to make the activities easily adaptable to your school's phonics program. These guidelines are not meant to be a full phonics program. In **every** case, use the phoneme and phonics cues that your phonics program recommends. See the chart below for specific information about the sounds presented in this series.

Vowel Sounds

These symbols encompass the sounds made by each combination of vowels and consonants. The letter combinations are paired with example words that make the sounds.

short /a/ and long /a/ • long /a/ includes ai as in rain, a_e as in cake, and ea as in break

short /e/ and long /e/ • short /e/ includes ea as in breath
- long /e/ includes ea as in steal, ee as in steel, ei as in either, ie as in thief, and y as in happy

short /i/ and long /i/ • short /i/ includes y as in myth (Note: some phonics programs deem ing as short /i/.)
- long /i/ includes ie as in tried, i_e as in ice, igh as in high, ight as in night, and y as in my

short /o/ and long /o/ • long /o/ includes oa as in goat, o_e as in role, ou as in soul, and ow as in slow

short /u/ and long /u/ • short /u/ includes oo as in blood
- long /u/ may include ew as in few, ou as in youth, ue as in blue, oo as in scoot (Different phonics programs consider either /yu/ and/or /oo/ as long /u/.)

Vowel Combinations, Vowel Teams, and Vowel-Consonant Teams

Difficult vowel combinations are treated individually. Each is paired with an example word that makes the sound.
- /au/ as in caught
- /oi/ and /oy/ as in poise and joy
- /ou/ and /ow/ as in loud and cow
- /aw/ as in saw (/au/ and /aw/ may differ depending on regional dialect)
- /oo/ as in spoon, foot, or short /u/ as in blood

R-Controlled Vowels and Diphthongs

Rather than substitute the *schwa* character (ə) for r-controlled vowels and diphthongs, they are listed with example words. This helps remind teachers to differentiate, for example, between the /or/ sound in the word *for* and the /or/ sound in the word *doctor*, so that students don't over-pronounce the *or* as doctOR or the *or* in *for* as *fur*. Additionally, many students who are learning to read find the schwa confusing in print and will learn the correct local pronunciation without additional coaching.

Consonant Sounds

/b/	/d/	/f/	/g/ (hard g as in goat)	/h/
/j/ (soft g as in gem)	/k/ (hard c as in cat)	/l/	/m/	/n/
/p/	/kw/ (for q with u)	/r/	/s/ (soft c as in cell)	/t/
/v/	/w/	/ks/ (x as in fox)	/y/	/z/

Digraphs

/ch/   /sh/ (ss as in mission, ch as in machine)   /th/ as in this (not voiced)
/th/ as in then (voiced)   /wh/ as in whale   /zh/ as in vision

Brown Bear, Brown Bear, What Do You See?

by Bill Martin, Jr.

(Holt, Rinehart, & Winston, 1967, 1983)

Learn what different-colored animals see in this rhyming book with predictable language. Its pattern makes it an excellent book for fluency practice, and for teaching the letter b, the /e/ sound, and color and animal words.

Related books: *A Color of His Own* by Leo Lionni (Knopf, 2000); *My Many Colored Days* by Dr. Seuss (Knopf, 1998); *Polar Bear, Polar Bear, What Do You Hear?* by Bill Martin, Jr. (Henry Holt & Company, 1997)

Phonemic Awareness Activities
for *Brown Bear, Brown Bear, What Do You See?*

Pre-reading Activity: Let students practice rhyming patterns and the long /e/ sound. Have students guess which two rhyming words they will hear over and over in the book. Give them a clue by telling them that one of the words is in the title. Once students determine that one of the words is *see*, help them guess its rhyming partner. Have students name words that rhyme with *see* until they suggest *me*. Explain that these words end with the long /e/ sound. Tell students that long vowel sounds make the letters say their names. Use the words *sheep, green,* and *teacher* from the book to teach words with medial (in the middle) long /e/ sounds. Have students think of other words that have the medial long /e/. Use the Long /E/ Sound reproducible (page 9) for assessment.

During-reading Activity: Ask students what sound the words *brown* and *bear* start with. Have them suggest other /b/ words. Read the title and ask how many times they hear /b/ (four). Ask students to guess how many times they will hear the /b/ sound in the book. List several guesses. As you read aloud, tell students to listen for and identify the /b/ sounds in the book by raising their hands or stomping their feet. Tally the number of /b/ phonemes in the book, then compare the actual number to the guesses. There are 26 /b/ sounds in the book, including the title and "/B/y /B/ill Martin Jr. and Pictures /b/y Eric Carle" on the title page.

Post-reading Activity: Explain that every time students open their mouths to form a word part, it is called a *syllable*. To reinforce this concept, have them place their fingers under their chins and read a few lines from the book aloud. Explain that each time their chins move, that is a syllable. Reread the book with students clapping the syllables, and again with students placing their fingers under their chins. Compare the number of syllables counted during the two readings. Reread the story title while students clap its syllables. Tell students to practice counting syllables in words from the story. Ask students to clap the syllable for *brown*. Repeat with other one-syllable words such as *bear, red, at, me,* etc. Ask students how many times they clap for *looking*. Repeat with two-syllable words *yellow, purple, goldfish, teacher,* and *children*.

Long /E/ Sound
phonemic awareness reproducible for
Brown Bear, Brown Bear, What Do You See?

Name_____ Date _____

Color the bears that have pictures with the long e sound like in the words *see* and *me*.

Phonics Activities
for *Brown Bear, Brown Bear, What Do You See?*

Pre-reading Activity: Have students say the following words: *the, me, see, teacher.* (Note that in many phonics programs, *the* is not considered a long /e/ word, but a word that ends with the schwa sound.) Ask students what those words have in common (the long /e/ sound). Write the words on the board and ask students what they notice about the letters that make the long /e/ sound. Help them see that ee, e, and ea can all make the long /e/ sound. Write e, ee, and ea on a piece of chart paper or the board to create three column headings. As a class, brainstorm a list of words that have the long /e/ sound, or use the list from the Long /E/ Sound reproducible (page 9). As students name words, list each word under its appropriate header. If you use a word wall in your classroom, add some of the simpler words to the word wall for future reference.

During-reading Activity: Provide a napkin or paper plate and a bowl of alphabet-shaped cereal or pasta, or small letter tiles for each student. Tell students that as they read the story, you will help them spell simple words with their letters. Read each page from the book. Pause to give students an opportunity to use sound spelling to spell a word from each page with their letters, using their napkins as "paper." Select the words to review specific phonics skills, or allow students to individually select some or all of the words. Some suggestions from the book might be color words, animal words, or other words in the repeated phrase. As students are spelling, observe their word-building skills, or have them tell you what words they are choosing. (Remember that students at this age will usually spell by sound, so expect invented spelling.) If students use cereal for this activity, make the game extra fun by giving them periodic opportunities to "eat their words."

Post-reading Activity: Take students on a classroom scavenger hunt to find things that begin with the letter b (as in *brown* and *bear*). (You may want to "plant" some b items for them to find in addition to everyday classroom items.) Have each student, pair, or small group walk around the room with a notepad and pencil, and look for things that begin with the letter b. When a student finds a b object, have him draw it and try writing its name on his paper. Give small prizes to students who find the most b objects. (Prizes should start with the letter b, of course!) Then, post students' illustrations on a bulletin board. Title the display, "Students, students, what b's did you see?" Use the Letter B reproducible (page 11) to assess students' letter recognition or provide further practice.

Name_____ Date _____

Say the name of each picture. If the name of the picture starts with the letter b, like bear, color it blue. If it starts with another letter, do not color the picture.

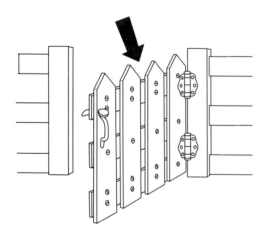

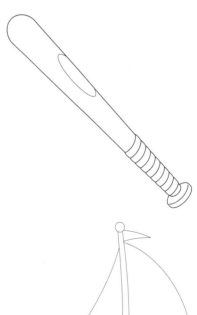

Vocabulary Activities

for *Brown Bear, Brown Bear, What Do You See?*

Pre-reading Activity: Create an animal word wall. On chart paper, write the animal names in the order in which they appear in the book (*bear, bird, duck, horse, frog, cat, dog, sheep, goldfish*). Point to each word and read it aloud. Have students repeat each word after you say it. Select nine student volunteers. Have each volunteer draw a picture of one animal on a sticky note. When each drawing is complete, have each student post his sticky note next to the correct animal and reread the word. After all of the illustrations are posted, have the class reread the list of animal words. Ask students to listen for these words as you read the story aloud. To use the word wall for assessment, cover the words and have students write them while looking at the pictures.

During-reading Activity: Write each color word from the story on a corresponding color of construction paper. For example, write the word *blue* on blue paper. Write large enough for the words to be legible from students' seats. Make enough color word cards for each student to have one. Ask each student to stand up when his color is read in the story (several students will stand up at once). Read the story, pausing when students stand up with their color word cards. Then, read each color word and have students repeat it. To extend the activity, post the color words and have students copy them using corresponding crayons, then add illustrations of colored objects, such as peas and frogs for green, apples and fire engines for red, etc. Post students' illustrations on a bulletin board with the color word cards.

Post-reading Activity: Use the Color Words Game reproducible (page 13) to give students practice reading color words. Have pairs of students cut out the game board and color and cut out a set of color word flash cards. On each flash card, have each pair color the rectangles to the right of the words. Give each student a game piece, such as a button, to place on the "Start" space. Have one player cover the colored part of a card, then "flash" just the word to the other player. The player who sees the card should name the color. When a player reads a word correctly, she should move her game piece one space forward. If a player does not read a word correctly, she should not move her game piece. The player who reaches the "finish line" first is the winner. Allow students to trade partners and play several times. For students who have memorized the color words, have them spell the words instead of naming them. For a kinesthetic variation, let each student use her body as game piece, and take one step forward on the floor when she reads or spells a color word correctly, until reaching a designated finish line.

Color Words Game

vocabulary reproducible for
Brown Bear, Brown Bear, What Do You See?

Name _____   Date _____

Cut out the game board and flash cards. Have your teacher tell you how to play the game.

Finish

Start

yellow

purple

gold

red

green

black

brown

blue

white

Fluency Activities
for *Brown Bear, Brown Bear, What Do You See?*

Pre-reading Activity: This is an excellent book for "chunking" because the text is already written with words grouped together. Tell students that chunking is the process of grouping words together as they read aloud because they "go" together. Write *Brown bear, brown bear* and *Yellow duck, yellow duck* or other story phrases on a piece of chart paper and read them aloud. Point out how the color word and animal name in each phrase are grouped or chunked together, so there should be no pause between the words when they are read aloud. The two words go together. Have students read them with you. Tell students that they will see this pattern throughout the book. Write the phrases *looking at me* and *What do you see?* on the chart. Read them aloud and discuss how these three or four words "sound right" when you chunk them. Have students read the phrases with you. Tell students to look for these phrases in the book and to practice chunking them when reading aloud.

During-reading Activity: This simple, repetitive book is a natural choice for dramatic play. Assign parts to students and let them perform the story. Provide art supplies and allow students to make puppets of the story animals from brown bags, or masks from paper plates and craft sticks. Have groups take turns reading the story aloud while using the puppets or masks. Praise fluent, expressive "actors." To encourage variation in tone, position students with consecutive parts at different distances from each other. Consider inviting parents or another class to watch the production.

Post-reading Activity: This activity can be done at a center while other students are working independently. After students are familiar with the book, record individual students reading the entire book or excerpts. Use this as one-on-one time to give students feedback about how fluently they read. Encourage students to track print (point to words as they read) to ensure they are following the text. Look for each student to demonstrate awareness of left-to-right progression as well as words and sentences. Play back each student's reading, praise his strengths, and give specific feedback on how to improve. For example, if a student reads all of the words correctly while pointing to them, but his reading is very choppy, say, "Walter, you did an excellent job pointing to the words as you read. You also got every word right! Next time I want you to work on grouping the words together so you sound more natural." Demonstrate areas in which you want students to improve by reading text back to them. If possible, keep a tape for each student and record his reading periodically so that you can both play back the tape and hear his improvements. Use the Fluency Assessment reproducible (page 15) to record results, notes, comments, and student progress.

Fluency Assessment
fluency reproducible for
Brown Bear, Brown Bear, What Do You See?

After recording and listening to a student read aloud, record information below. Use a fluency rating of 1–3 to assess overall fluency 1=reads smoothly and with good expression, pausing when appropriate; 2=is somewhat fluent (exhibits some fluency characteristics but needs to improve on others); 3=choppy, uneven reading, pauses inappropriately, sounds "robotic."

Student Name	Date	Fluency Rating	Comments

Pre-reading Activity: Prepare students to read the book and discover personal connections to the literature by having them write "what they see" on the Here's What I See reproducible (page 17). Give each student several copies of the Here's What I See reproducible. Instruct students to observe and record things they see on their way home from school, or at a grocery store, in their backyards, etc. As they make observations, have students fill in the blanks on the reproducibles and illustrate what they see. If you have beginning writers, ask parents to write or record what students dictate to them in place of having students write. Encourage students to get help from family members to label their drawings, also. Call on students using the book's pattern (for example: "Bernard, Bernard, what did you see?"), and have them share observations with the class.

During-reading Activity: Give each student a sentence strip. Tell students that they will be recording the events of the story in order to retell it later. As you read, pause long enough after each page to give students time to illustrate the animal described on that page. For example, after you read the first page, have students draw brown bears. Remind students to begin on the left and work towards the right, the same way they would write. When the drawings are complete, let students practice retelling the story to partners using their "notes" as reminders.

Post-reading Activity: At the beginning of the school year, read *Brown Bear, Brown Bear, What Do You See?* aloud to the class. Then, use the book to help students learn each other's names. For example, you may call out "Bethany, Bethany, who do you see?" Bethany would respond, "I see Pablo looking at me." Then, Bethany should ask, "Pablo, Pablo…" and so on. Continue until all student names are called. Read the book and repeat the exercise every day until students know their classmates' names. Finally, ask if anyone in the class can recite the book from memory. Talk about which is more difficult, remembering their classmates' names or the names of characters in the book.

Here's What I See

Name_____   Date _____

Choose a place you visit often, such as a park, your yard, a grocery store, or another place. Draw some things you see. Fill in the blanks with the names of the objects you draw.

I see _____.   I see _____.

I see _____.   I see _____.

Chicka Chicka Boom Boom

by Bill Martin, Jr. and John Archambault

(Simon & Schuster Books for Young Readers, 1989)

What happens when 26 lowercase letters decide to climb a coconut tree? Boom Boom is the answer! All of the uppercase letters rush to the rescue of their small counterparts in this rhyming alphabet book. This book definitely gives the impression that the letters that make up the English language are lively!

Related books: *A My Name is Alice* by Jane Bayer (Dutton, 1992); *ABC I Like Me!* by Nancy L. Carlson (Puffin, 1999); *The Alphabet Tree* by Leo Lionni (Knopf, 1990); *Dr. Seuss's ABC* (I Can Read It All by Myself Beginner Books) by Dr. Seuss (Random House, 1996); *The Letters Are Lost!* by Lisa Campbell Ernst (Puffin, 1999); *A Long Trip to Z* by Fulvio Testa (Harcourt Brace, 1997)

Phonemic Awareness Activities
for *Chicka Chicka Boom Boom*

Pre-reading Activity: Provide a review for students who have already learned the sounds of letters in the alphabet or simply expose students to phonemes prior to reading the book. Create and display a paper coconut tree on a bulletin board. Add lowercase letters of the alphabet (put letters that don't fit on the tree next to it or on the "ground"). As you post each letter, say its sound or sounds. Have students name objects that begin with the sound or sounds that the letter makes. Then, let each student draw and attach a picture of one of the objects under its letter on the tree. If 26 letters will not fit, change the letters and pictures every few days.

During-reading Activity: Tell students that rhyming words are words that have the same ending sounds, like *tree, me,* and *see.* List other words that rhyme with these words. Tell students to listen for rhyming words in the book as you read aloud. Explain that whenever students hear a rhyming word, they should "boom" like the coconut tree. Pause periodically as you read to praise or correct "booms." You may also want to chant "boom" as you and students listen to a recording of the book. Use the Boom Boom reproducible (page 19) to assess students' knowledge or provide further practice. (Read the picture names and sounds on the reproducible for students.)

Post-reading Activity: The word *boom* is easy to pronounce, and it is often repeated in the book, so use it for a phoneme manipulation exercise. Help students hear that oom is what is left when you remove the /b/ sound from the word *boom* in the story. Ask students what the word *boom* would turn into if you changed the beginning phoneme to /f/ (*foom*). Experiment with different initial phonemes to make real and nonsense words like *room, doom,* and *moom.* To energize students' letter-sound recognition practice, hold up consonant flash cards and let the class shout the words created with the *oom* sound and each new consonant.

First-Rate Reading™ Grade K • CD-0068 • © Carson-Dellosa

Boom Boom

phonemic awareness reproducible for
Chicka Chicka Boom Boom

Name _____ Date _____

Listen as your teacher says the name of each picture and reads the sounds in the trees. Draw a line from each picture to the coconut tree with the rhyming sound.

an   ee   at

Phonics Activities
for *Chicka Chicka Boom Boom*

Pre-reading Activity: Introduce students to the letter characters in *Chicka Chicka Boom Boom* by singing "The Alphabet Song" with the class. As they sing each letter, have students point to the corresponding letter on a chart or poster. Provide a set of 26 index cards. Program each card with one letter (one uppercase and lowercase letter per card), or use a box of alphabet flash cards. Randomly distribute the cards to students. Have students hold their letter cards, stand up, and arrange themselves in alphabetical order. Reread (or sing) the alphabet using students' letter cards as a guide this time. For an extra challenge, have students remain in random order. As you sing each letter, have the student with that letter hold up his card. Hold up the appropriate letter cards as you sing the alphabet song. Rotate letters and repeat.

During-reading Activity: Prior to this activity, gather a class supply of containers such as shoe boxes, lids with sides that are at least two inches (five centimeters) tall, plastic containers, etc., and fill them with small amounts of sand. If it is not possible to provide each student with a sandbox, prepare a center with one or two sandboxes and a copy of *Chicka Chicka Boom Boom*. Provide small, plastic combs for "erasing," to discourage students from shaking the containers. Remind students that coconut trees often grow in sand. Tell them that maybe the letters left impressions in the sand when they fell! (Press your finger into clay to show a concrete example of the word *impression*.) As you read the story aloud, have students trace the alphabet letters from the book in their own sandboxes. Pause as you read the story aloud, giving students an opportunity to form each letter as it appears in the text. Have students comb the sand after each letter to prepare for the next one, or let them write the group of letters mentioned on each page next to each other in the sand.

Post-reading Activity: Give each student a copy of the All Fall Down reproducible (page 21). Explain that some of the alphabet letters have fallen out of the coconut tree again. Have each student cut out the fallen letters and paste them in the correct order on the tree. To create a center activity, attach a large, paper trunk to a bulletin board or wall and add felt leaves. Program index cards with one letter each, and attach hook-and-loop tape to the backs of the cards. Let students practice attaching the letters to the felt leaves in order.

All Fall Down

phonics reproducible for
Chicka Chicka Boom Boom

Name_____ Date _____

Oh no! The letters fell out of the coconut tree! Cut out the letters at the bottom of the page. Paste them on the tree in the correct order.

| a | b | | d | e | | g | | i | j | |

| l | m | n | o | | q | r | | t | u |

| v | | x | y | |

| c | h | k | f | s | p | w | z |

Vocabulary Activities
for *Chicka Chicka Boom Boom*

Pre-reading Activity: Tell students that sometimes authors use nonsense words in their books just for fun. Say the following words in random order and have students determine if they are nonsense words or "real" words: *skit, skat, skoodle, doot, flee, chicka, tree, coconut, flop, flip, boom.* Tell students to listen for nonsense words in the story. (The words *chicka* and *whee* can be included with the other words at this point, but see the following activity for a more specific lesson on these words.) The words *looped, stooped,* and the phrase *wiggle-jiggle* are excellent examples of how "real" words can be used in nonsensical ways. Challenge students to come up with their own nonsense words. Write some of these words on the board and have students chant them or make up silly meanings for them.

During-reading Activity: Explain that authors often use noise words to help readers "hear" what is going on. (Students will probably love learning and saying the word *onomatopoeia*!) Tell students to find "noise words" in the story (*chicka, boom, whee*) while you read aloud. Ask students to indicate when they hear a noise word by repeating that noise. See the post-reading activity for an extension.

Post-reading Activity: To continue the during-reading activity, work on more sound words. After reading, brainstorm other "noise words" (*splat, splash, crunch, vroom*) and talk about what kinds of things might make these noises. Celebrate the sounds words make by creating a class onomatopoeia book. Bring in several objects that make noise such as bubble wrap, cellophane, a box of cornstarch (squeeze it to make the noise), a bell, a small percussion instrument, etc. Let students experiment with the objects to hear their noises. Have each student write and illustrate a copy of the Words That Make Noise reproducible (page 23). For example, one student may illustrate *"Plip plip!" went the water drop.* You may need to help beginning writers with letter formation and spelling. Students can use invented spelling, copy words from the board after a brainstorming session, or dictate their sounds to you. When the pages are complete, record each student reading her page and making the accompanying noise. Bind the pages to create a class book. Place the tape and book in a center with all of the noisemakers, so that students get to experiment with different noise words and sounds. Consider displaying this project at an open house or parents' night.

Words That Make Noise

vocabulary reproducible for
Chicka Chicka Boom Boom

Name_____ Date _____

Choose an object and listen carefully to the sound that it makes. Fill in the blanks in the bottom sentence, and draw a picture that shows the object making its noise.

"<u>Boom Boom</u>!" went the coconut tree.

"_____!" went the _____.

Fluency Activities

for *Chicka Chicka Boom Boom*

Pre-reading Activity: Use the Chant with Me reproducible (page 25) to practice fluency and "chunking" words together. Distribute copies to students and enlarge a copy of the reproducible for your use. Read the chant aloud to students. Point out how you chunked or grouped certain words together in order for the chant to sound "good" and make sense. For example, say, "See how when I read it, I grouped the words *I went up* and *the coconut tree* together? Wouldn't it have sounded strange if I read it: I went [pause] up the coconut [pause] tree?" Explain that good readers try to sound natural when they read aloud—the way they do when they talk. Emphasize that although a chant is read in rhythm which sounds different from talking, regular conversation has a rhythm as well. Reread the chant, this time emphasizing the chunking of the words as you point to them on the enlarged copy. Have students use their fingers or pencils to point to the words as they read the chant. Or, have students work in pairs. Have one partner point to the words while the other reads and vice versa.

During-reading Activity: This book naturally lends itself to echo reading because of the chanting pattern. Tell students what an echo is, and have them practice echoing by repeating some of the noises or words you say. Read the story aloud, pausing where appropriate, then have the class echo you. Praise students who use the same expression or fluidity you used as you read. As students become more comfortable with the book, point to students and let them echo your reading one at a time. Reward fluent readers by having small groups lead the echo.

Post-reading Activity: Have students read the book aloud and perform for the class, parents, visitors, etc. This can be done in many ways and is great fun! One variation is to assign "character parts" to students while you serve as the narrator. For example, have one student be "A" and another "B." You read "A told B, and B told C" then the two students continue "I'll meet you at the top of the coconut tree" (*Chicka Chicka Boom Boom*, page 1). Another possibility is to assign parts or pages of the book to groups of students as you guide them through the reading. Decide on ways to act out story parts. Students can jump up for "Chicka chicka," wiggle hips for "boom boom," wrap their arms around themselves for "and uncles and aunts hug their little dears" (*Chicka Chicka Boom Boom*, page 13), etc. Then, rehearse the movements as students read the story aloud. Invite parents for a "Chicka Boom Party," and have students perform and read the story. To complete the theme, let students create letter necklaces, name tags, T-shirts, etc., to use as costumes.

Name_____ Date _____

Use a pencil or your finger to track the print as you read.

Chicka chicka boom boom.

Chicka chicka boom.

Who went up the coconut tree?

I went up the coconut tree.

Chicka chicka boom boom.

Chicka chicka boom.

Who fell down the coconut tree?

I fell down the coconut tree.

Chicka chicka boom boom.

Chicka chicka boom.

Yes, it was me!

Me! Me! Me!

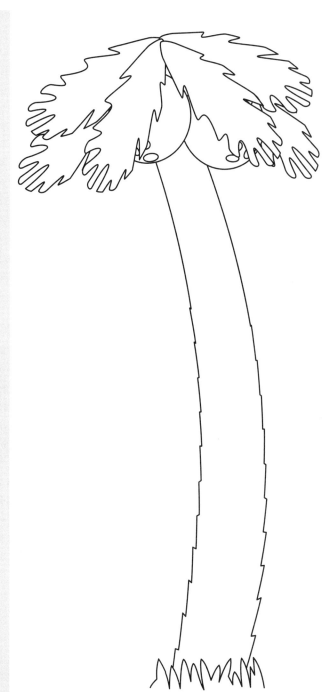

Comprehension Activities
for *Chicka Chicka Boom Boom*

Pre-reading Activity: To establish prior knowledge for students, ask, "Have you ever climbed a tree? What might happen if you climb a tree? Have you ever seen a coconut? Where do coconuts grow? Who might climb a coconut tree?" If possible, show pictures of a coconut tree and bring in a real coconut to share. (Many supermarkets sell shelled coconuts.) Then, tell students that they will be reading a story about the alphabet letters climbing a coconut tree. If you have pictures of a coconut tree available, talk about why it might be difficult to climb this type of tree. (There are no branches to hold onto while climbing.)

During-reading Activity: Tell students that good readers think while they read. This is called "active reading" because their brains should be active, or "on," at the same time that they are listening to (or reading) a story. Help students listen and think about what is happening at the beginning, in the middle, and at the end of *Chicka Chicka Boom Boom*. Give each student a copy of the Sequencing reproducible (page 27). After you have read the pages in which the alphabet goes up the tree, pause and ask students to summarize what has happened in the story so far. After doing this orally, have each student illustrate what has happened in the first coconut. Continue reading and pause again after the letters fall down. Ask students to summarize and illustrate what happened next in the story. Repeat until the story is complete and students have identified what happened at the beginning, in the middle, and at the end.

Post-reading Activity: In order to truly understand text, students must be able to understand lower-order and higher-order questions. Lower-order questions have answers that can literally be found in the text, while higher-order questions require students to make inferences and connections to find the answers. Have informal discussions with small groups of students. Allow them to respond to the following lower- and higher-order questions orally, by dictating their answers for you to write, or in illustration form.

Lower order: "Who climbed the tree? What kind of tree did the letters climb? What did D say to E, F, and G? What happened when the whole alphabet went up the tree?"

Higher order: "Why do you think the letters wanted to climb the tree? Do you think any of the letters were scared to climb the tree? If so, which ones and why? What did the letters do at the top of the tree? What do you think will happen if they climb the tree again? Who do you think will take A's dare at the end? What would you do if someone dared you to climb a tree?"

Name_____ Date _____

Draw what happened in the beginning of the story.

Draw what happened in the middle of the story.

Draw what happened at the end of the story.

Corduroy
by Don Freeman

(Viking, 1968)

Corduroy has been sitting on the toy department shelf for a long time. A little girl wants him, but her mother says he's missing a button and they have spent enough money that day. Corduroy looks for his lost button overnight but instead finds a friend. Use this book to teach fluency, synonyms, and more advanced phonics skills.

Related books: *Corduroy Goes to School* by B. G. Hennessy (Viking Children's Books, 2002); *Corduroy's Party* by Don Freeman (Viking Press, 1985); *A Pocket for Corduroy* by Don Freeman (Viking Press, 1980)

Phonemic Awareness Activities
for *Corduroy*

Pre-reading Activity: Give each student a button. Say it's a clue about the story. Ask students to say the word *button* and listen to the phonemes. Ask, "What sound do you hear at the beginning of the word *button*? What sound do you hear in the middle of *button*? At the end?" Help students identify the /b/, /t/, and /n/ sounds. Ask what letters represent those sounds. Explain that it is important to pay attention to the beginning, middle, and ending sounds of words. Have students identify beginning, middle, and ending phonemes in words such as *rabbit, hammer, kitten, lemon, zipper, butter,* etc. Help students complete the Middle and Ending Phonemes reproducible (page 29) for more practice.

During-reading Activity: Write the word *Corduroy* on the board. Have students sound it out. Ask, "Why does the letter o make different sounds in the first and last syllables?" Explain that in both cases, the letter o is being influenced by the letter after it. In the first syllable, the o is r-controlled. In the last syllable, the o makes a diphthong (new sound) with the letter y. Orally compare those two sounds with short /o/ and long /o/. As you come to similar words during the reading, such as *morning* and *for*, stop and let students sound them out. Write similar words on the board. Use the pre-reading phonics activity (page 30) for more practice with the oy diphthong.

Post-reading Activity: Manipulatives can make counting more concrete for young students. Give each student a paper plate and a handful of bear-shaped gummy candy in a paper cup to use to practice counting syllables. Say a word from the book. Ask each student to show the number of syllables in that word by placing a candy on her plate to represent each syllable. For example, if you ask how many syllables are in the word *bear*, each student should place one candy on her plate. After students have finished the activity, allow them to eat their "answers." Some words to try are *Corduroy, Lisa, overalls, button, lost, store, toy, department, escalator,* and *friend*.

First-Rate Reading™ Grade K • CD-0068 • © Carson-Dellosa

Middle and Ending Phonemes

phonemic awareness reproducible for
Corduroy

Name _____   Date _____

As your teacher says the name of each picture, listen for the middle sound and the ending sound. Write the letter that names the middle sound and the letter that names the ending sound under each picture.

middle sound _____   middle sound _____   middle sound _____

ending sound _____   ending sound _____   ending sound _____

middle sound _____   middle sound _____   middle sound _____

ending sound _____   ending sound _____   ending sound _____

Phonics Activities
for *Corduroy*

Pre-reading Activity: Use this activity to help students further understand the concept of diphthongs. Show the book cover to students and tell them that the story is about a toy bear named Corduroy. Write the words *Corduroy* and *toy* on the board. Have students repeat them. Ask students what the two words have in common (oy). Explain that when two letters blend together to make a new sound, it is called a *diphthong*. Tell students that the /oy/ phoneme in these words is called a diphthong. Students will enjoy repeating this peculiar word! Label a piece of chart paper with four columns: oy, oi, ou, ow. Help students sound out each diphthong and discuss how in each instance the two letters make a new sound now that they are together. Also, have students notice that the first two and last two diphthongs make the same sounds but are spelled differently. Write each of the following words on an index card: *crown, owl, mouse, Corduroy, cloud, cow, oyster, coin, boy, blouse, toy, soil, mouth, about, enjoy, shout, down, point, voice, howl, loud, noun, clown, noise.* Give one card to each student. If necessary, repeat some words or write extra words to ensure that every student gets a card. Have students hold their cards and stand up as you walk around the room and read each card. After you read a card, have the student repeat the word, and then have the class repeat it. Ask the student holding the card to go up to the chart and place the card in the correct column according to its diphthong. Ask the rest of the class to check to see if she is right, and either agree or disagree with her answer. If she places the card in the wrong column, have her move the card to the correct column. When the student places the card in the correct column, ask her to point to the diphthong in her word and isolate the sound. Continue until all cards are placed in the correct columns. See the during-reading activity below for more diphthong work.

During-reading Activity: This activity extends the pre-reading activity above. Assign each student one of the following diphthongs: oy, oi, ou, ow. Provide copies of *Corduroy* at a center. Have students count the number of times they see their assigned diphthong in the text while reading. Be prepared for questions about the words *going* and *should.* Have students write the words in which they found their diphthongs and underline the diphthongs. After each student has had a turn, divide the class into groups according to assigned diphthongs. Have students count diphthongs in the text together to check their findings. Then, compile the groups' findings to make a class chart, and discuss as a class which diphthong was found most often in *Corduroy.*

Post-reading Activity: Brainstorm with students what could have happened to Corduroy's button. Ask students, "How did he lose it? Where did it go? How did it fall?" Have students call out where they think the button might be. However, tell them that the places all have to start with the letter b. For example: *in the bed, in the boys' clothing section, in the bathroom,* etc. On the board, draw a button to be the middle of a web. As students provide responses, list them on the web. Then, have each student use a copy of the Where Is Corduroy's Button? reproducible (page 31) to write one possibility of what happened to the button, and illustrate it. Display the illustrations on a bulletin board titled "Where Could My Button Be?"

Name_____ Date _____

Where could Corduroy's button be? Think of an answer that begins with the letter b. Write your answer on the lines. Draw a picture of your answer inside the button.

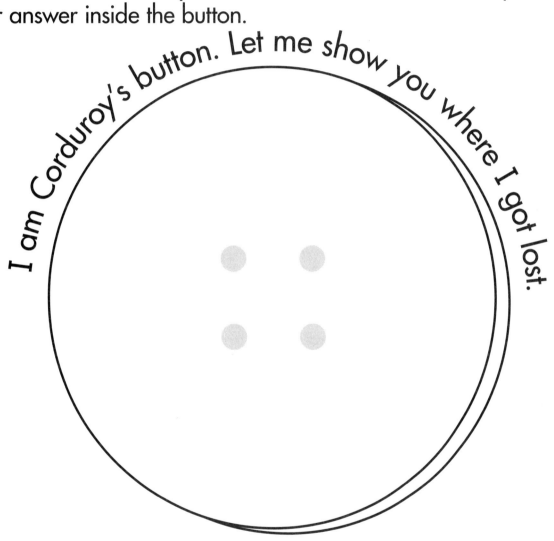

I am Corduroy's button. Let me show you where I got lost.

Corduroy's button is _____

_____.

Vocabulary Activities
for *Corduroy*

Pre-reading Activity: Tell students that sometimes you can change a word slightly by adding letters to the end, such as wait/waited or buy/buying. When you add something to the end of a word it is called a *suffix*. Explain that sometimes you have to add a suffix, because otherwise the word would not "sound right" in the sentence. Write the sentence *Yesterday I jump in the park.* on the board and read it aloud. Ask students if the sentence sounds right, and what they should do to make it sound right (add ed to jump). Reread the sentence with the suffix added and ask if it sounds right. Help students practice reading suffix words from the story. Write each of the following words on an index card: *wait, fill, watch, buy, search, move, admire.* Add more words if necessary. Program index cards with the ed and ing suffixes, and tell students that these are only two of many suffixes. Give each student a word or suffix card. Have students with base word cards stand up one at a time and hold them. Read each word aloud and have students repeat the word. Then, have the suffix cardholders try joining their cards, one at a time, to the base word card to see if the suffix makes a new word. Have students read the new words aloud (*waited, filled, watched, buying, searching, moving, admiring*) as they are formed. Show students that the letter e disappears when adding these suffixes by having the suffix card holders cover the e when adding the suffix cards to *move* and *admire.* Tell students to look for these words and other ed and ing words in the story.

During-reading Activity: Some words in the text will be new or unfamiliar to students, such as *sighed, escalator, admiring, toppled, dashing,* and *fastened.* To help students learn these new words in context, pause to discuss them as you read the book. Guide students toward using picture clues and story clues to figure out what the words mean. For example, ask students, "What do you think toppled means? If we look at the picture to get a clue, we see that Corduroy is falling off the bed and onto the floor. And, the sentence says, '. . . and off the mattress Corduroy toppled' " (*Corduroy*, page 18). "So, what do you suppose toppled means?" After students make guesses about each word, share the correct definitions.

Post-reading Activity: Tell students that good writers use interesting words. Find the following words in the story: *sighed, wandered, toppled, dashing, enormous.* As you find each word, reread the sentence containing the word and discuss what the word means. Have students think of other words that would mean the same thing as that word (such as *fell* for *toppled*). List the word with its synonyms on a piece of chart paper. Tell students that words that mean the same thing are called *synonyms.* Discuss why the author might have chosen these specific words instead of others that would mean the same thing (*sighed* and *gasped* instead of *said*, etc.). Then, give students copies of the Synonym Sampler reproducible (page 33). As students work on the worksheets, read the directions, sentences, and possible answers aloud to help students who have a difficult time reading longer words.

Name _____ Date _____

Listen as your teacher reads the sentences and words aloud. Then, circle the word that has the same meaning as each underlined word.

1. Corduroy was a bear who lived in a toy <u>shop</u>.

   store   shelf

2. Corduroy was <u>sad</u>.

   angry   unhappy

3. Corduroy's button was <u>missing</u>.

   lost   broken

4. Corduroy looked for his button while the other toys were <u>sleeping</u>.

   napping   playing

5. Corduroy <u>wished</u> for a home.

   wanted   built

6. Lisa and Corduroy became great <u>pals</u>.

   toys   friends

Fluency Activities
for *Corduroy*

Pre-reading Activity: One of the problems that many young readers have with fluency is that they pronounce words phonetically—the way they learned them—while reading. A common example is that students will say "lit-tle" with the hard emphasis on the medial t's, making the word sound choppy. This book is an excellent tool for unlearning this habit, because the word *button* reappears so often in the text. Hold up a button and ask students to identify it. When students say "button," respond, "Yes, it's a button. Do we say but-ton when we are speaking, or do we say button?" Display some other words on the board to read, such as *mitten, kitten, ladder,* and *party*. Ask students to read the words in a fluent, natural manner, the way they would say them if they were talking. Remind them that it is important to read words like they would say them when talking to a friend.

During-reading Activity: When writing the characters' dialogue, this author uses many words other than the word said, such as *sighed, gasped, cried,* and *wondered*. As you read, pause at these words, and point them out to students. For example, tell students, "You see how the author wrote sighed instead of just said? The author did that so you know when you are reading how the mother sounds when she says that to Lisa. She sighs, like she's really tired or sad." Reread the character's dialogue, emphasizing the *sighing*. Repeat this in other words from the text, such as when Corduroy *wondered* where his lost button went and the watchman *exclaimed* about who toppled the lamp.

Post-reading Activity: Because this book has a large amount of dialogue, it is an excellent tool to practice fluency and expressive reading. Tell students that it is especially important to sound natural when you read a book that has dialogue (characters talking to each other). Reread some of the dialogue from the book, and ask students to notice how you sound as if you were really participating in a conversation. Use the My New Toy Bear reproducible (page 35) to practice reading dialogue fluently. Copy the reproducible onto a transparency, or enlarge it to poster size and laminate it. Read it chorally several times with students, and help them recognize words they do not know. Then, write different students' names on the blanks with a write-on/wipe-away marker. Read chorally until each student has her name read aloud by the class. For extra practice, give a copy of the reproducible to each student to take home.

My New Toy Bear

fluency reproducible for
Corduroy

Name_____   Date _____

Write a friend's name in the blanks labeled with a 1. Write your name in the blanks labeled with a 2. Then, use these sentences to practice reading aloud.

"Hey, _____ ! Do you want to see my new toy bear?"
            1

asked _____ .
          2

"Oh, yes!" cried _____ . "Let me see!"
               1

"It's brand new," explained _____ proudly.
                    2

"Wow," admired _____ . "It is so cute."
             1

"Thank you. I really love it!" said _____ .
                      2

"I wish I had a new toy bear," sighed _____ .
                         1

Comprehension Activities
for *Corduroy*

Pre-reading Activity: Consider recruiting a parent volunteer for this activity. Have students prepare to read the story by bringing in their favorite stuffed toys to share with the class. Have students complete copies of the My Toy Story reproducible (page 37). Have each student tell the name of his stuffed toy, describe what it looks like, tell the story of how he got it, and explain why it's his favorite. (Use a parent volunteer or teaching assistant to help you write students' dictated answers since many students cannot write at this age.) After students have completed their worksheets, have everyone sit in a circle with their stuffed toys. Have students take turns reading their answers and showing their toys. Students may need help remembering what they said, so prompt them if necessary. Tell students to compare their toy stories with the book when you read it. After reading *Corduroy* aloud to students, have the class help you complete a worksheet from the character Lisa's perspective.

During-reading Activity: This activity monitors comprehension, makes students read actively, and also has them focus on details. Tell students that Corduroy wants something in the book, but he is not really sure of what he has always wanted until the very end. Have students help you keep track of the things that Corduroy says he wants throughout the book by drawing pictures. Before you begin reading, give each student a piece of drawing paper and crayons or markers. As you read aloud, pause when Corduroy is going up the escalator and says he thinks he's always wanted to climb a mountain. Ask students, "What does Corduroy think he wants so far?" Have them draw mountains on their drawing paper. Continue reading and pause again when Corduroy guesses he has always wanted a palace. Have each student draw a palace. Ask students what words Corduroy uses to make readers think he is not sure that he really wants to climb a mountain or to live in a palace (*think, guess*). Tell students to keep listening to see if Corduroy finds something he wants. To allow students time to draw, pause again when he finds other things, such as a mattress, a home, and a friend. Afterwards, have students share their drawings and discuss which things Corduroy kind of wanted and which things he really wanted. Ask students if Corduroy got what he wanted, then let students name some things they really want.

Post-reading Activity: Discuss the fantasy elements present in the story. Ask students, "Could this story really happen? What parts are real? What parts are make-believe?" Have students list which elements could happen and which could not really happen. Then, lead the class to imagine what happens when all of the toys in the department are awake and no one is watching. Have students write (or dictate) and illustrate stories that tell what happens when the toys are awake.

 First-Rate Reading™ Grade K • CD-0068 • © Carson-Dellosa

My Toy Story

comprehension reproducible for
Corduroy

Name_____ Date _____

Fill in the blanks to tell about your favorite stuffed toy.

My _____ 's name is _____ .

This is what my _____ looks like: _____

_____

_____

_____

_____

This is the story of how I got my _____ .

_____

_____

_____

_____

_____

It is my favorite because _____

_____

_____

Goodnight Moon
by Margaret Wise Brown

(HarperCollins Juvenile Books, 1975)

This classic bedtime book tells the story of a little rabbit who is getting ready to go to sleep and is wishing a good night to objects in the room. The book has a gentle rhyming pattern with simple text and descriptive pictures, and is excellent for word recognition and the letter g.

Related books: And *If the Moon Could Talk* by Kate Banks (Farrar, Straus & Giroux, 1998); *Guess How Much I Love You* by Sam McBratney (Candlewick Press, 1996); *My World* by Margaret Wise Brown (HarperFestival, 2003); *The Runaway Bunny* by Margaret Wise Brown (HarperFestival, 1991); *There's an Alligator Under My Bed* by Mercer Mayer (Dutton, 1987)

Phonemic Awareness Activities
for *Goodnight Moon*

Pre-reading Activity: Read the title aloud and ask what sound is at the beginning of the word *goodnight*. Say the word, stressing the hard /g/ sound and have students repeat it. Identify the sound as /g/. Repeat this exercise with the word *giraffe*. Tell students that the /g/ sound at the beginning of *goodnight* is called the hard g, while the soft /g/ sound (as in *giraffe*) is called the soft g. Give each student a rock and a feather or cotton ball. Tell students to hold up a rock when they hear a hard /g/ in a word and to hold up a feather when they hear a soft /g/ in a word. Call out or show pictures of hard /g/ and soft /g/ words, such as great, green, good, gorilla, giraffe, gym, gentle, giant. Have students repeat the words, stressing the /g/ sound, and hold up the rock or feather. Help pairs practice using copies of the Letter G Sounds reproducible (page 39). (There is also a silent g in *goodnight*. Consider introducing it if students ask questions or seem otherwise ready for it.)

During-reading Activity: Review initial phoneme identification. Write the following letters on index cards (one letter per card): m, t, r, b, p, j, l, s, k, y, f, w, h. Make enough cards to distribute one to every student, repeating letters if needed. Read the story and have students listen for words that begin with sounds made by the consonants on their cards. When each student hears her assigned sound, have her raise her card and call out the phoneme sound ("b-b-b!"). Stop reading, have the student identify the word she heard with that phoneme. Then, have the class repeat the word and isolate the beginning phoneme.

Post-reading Activity: Practice syllable identification with this very simple text. Have students close their eyes. Read the story aloud slowly and have students make a snoring sound each time they hear a syllable. For example, when you read "And goodnight mittens" (*Goodnight Moon*, page 5), students should snore five times.

Letter G Sounds

phonemic awareness reproducible for
Goodnight Moon

Your Partner's Name _____   Date _____

Work with a partner. Say the name of each picture. Let your partner say "rock" for hard g like in goat, or "feather" for soft g like in gym. Look for the circle around a rock or a feather to check your partner's answers.

gingerbread man

gorilla

guitar

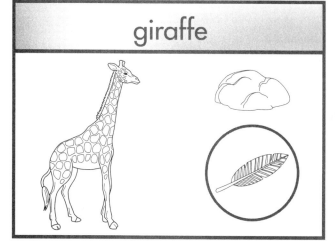

giraffe

goose

Phonics Activities
for *Goodnight Moon*

Pre-reading Activity: This activity correlates to the phonemic awareness pre-reading activity (page 38). Prepare a chart with one column for hard g words and another for soft g words. Attach a small rock and a feather or cotton ball to the appropriate sides of the chart to provide students with visual cues for hard and soft. Help students preview the book and find all of the words containing the letter g. List these words according to hard or soft g. All of the words will be either hard g or silent g, so you may wish to draw a column for silent g, like the second g in *goodnight*, since students will be looking for the letter g, rather than looking for the sounds. Then, brainstorm and list other words that begin with the letter g. Use the G Words reproducible (page 41) for assessment. Read both directions and words to students, and model printing the letter g beforehand.

During-reading Activity: The simple text in *Goodnight Moon* provides students with word recognition practice. Copy the text on sentence strips and cut the sentences into separate words. Randomly distribute the words to students and help them cut apart their words into letters. Have students practice spelling the words and saying the letter sounds. Instruct students to listen for their words as you read the book aloud. When a student hears her word being read, have her raise her word in the air and wait until you are finished reading that page (so it doesn't interfere with the reading). When you finish reading the page, call on students whose hands are raised. Have them come to the front of the classroom and identify the letters and sounds in their words.

Post-reading Activity: Students need to practice writing words, sounding out letters, forming graphemes, etc., by using real writing activities so that they can apply what they have learned. Review the things that the rabbit says good night to. Ask students to think of what they might say good night to when they get ready for bed in their own rooms. Tell students that they will help you write sentences telling different things good night. At the top of a piece of chart paper, write *Goodnight* _____. (Use good night if you want to use the correct spelling, or keep it as one word to follow the book exactly.) Have students fill in the blank with people and things they might tell good night. As students respond, guide them to help you write the sentences. For example, this activity may look like this conversation.

Teacher: "What else might you say good night to?"
Student: "My dog."
Teacher: "OK, can you help me write that?" (Begin writing on the chart.) "Good night…What letter do you think *dog* starts with? D-d-dog."
Students: "D!"
Teacher: "That's right. *D-d-dog* starts with the letter d." (Continue writing.) "What letter do you think is next? Do-o-o-g?" etc.

When you have let each student contribute a sentence, have students pick a few sentences to copy and illustrate on paper. Allowing them to write will reinforce phonics practice and make it more concrete.

G Words
phonics reproducible for
Goodnight Moon

Name_____ Date _____

The letter g can make the hard g sound like the g at the beginning of goodnight. The letter g can also make the soft g sound like the g at the beginning of giraffe. Write a letter g on each line. Then, listen as your teacher reads the words. Circle the rock if it makes a hard g sound. Circle the feather if it makes a soft g sound.

__ate

__orilla

__em

__oose

__ingerbread

__oat

__erbil

__iraffe

__irl

Vocabulary Activities
for *Goodnight Moon*

Pre-reading Activity: Before this activity, write each word in a compound word, such as *up/stairs*, *down/stairs*, *class/room*, etc. on pieces of sentence strip. With the class, write the word *goodnight* on a sentence strip and display it in a pocket chart. Ask students how many words are in the pocket (1), and how they know it is only one word (there is no extra space between any of the letters). Cut the sentence strip in half and display *good* and *night* with a space in between. Ask how many words are now in the pocket chart, then have them explain how they know there are two words (because there is space between the words). Have each student use the word *good* in a sentence. Repeat with the word *night*. Next, ask each student to use the word *goodnight* in a sentence. (If students notice that this is not how *good night* is usually spelled, simply explain that the author put the two words together just for this book.) Tell students that words that are made up of two words put together are called *compound words*. Have two students stand up to hold the pieces of sentence strips with the compound word parts. Have the students stand separately. Read the two separate words as a class. Then, have the two students come together to form the compound word. Ask the class what new word the two words make. Repeat for all compound words.

During-reading Activity: Introduce the positional words *over* and *under* by asking students to sit under their desks, jump over something, etc. Tell students that they will use positional words to find things in the story's illustrations. As you read, pause at each page and ask students to find items named in the text. For example, ask, "Where is the red balloon? Is it over or under the bed?" Have them use positional words to indicate where each item is located. Turn this into a game by having students guess what item from the page you are describing based on positional clues. For example, say "I see something that is under the sheets." or "I see something that is over the fireplace." Let students who understand these two positional words provide positional word clues while the rest of the class guesses. Use the Over and Under reproducible with individuals or small groups (page 43) for assessment. Provide a copy of the reproducible and a red and a blue crayon for each student. Read the following instructions aloud, then collect students' papers.

- Color the mitten that is under the table red. Color the mitten that is over the table blue.
- Color the balloon that is under the window red. Color the balloon that is over the window blue.
- Color the mouse that is over the bed blue. Color the mouse that is under the bed red.
- Color the bunny that is over the blanket blue. Color the bunny that is under the blanket red.

Post-reading Activity: Teach related vocabulary by asking students at what time of day the story takes place (night). Ask students to name the opposite of night. If students have not learned opposites yet, say, "When it is not night, it is ___." Write the words *day* and *night* at the top of a piece of chart paper. Ask students to brainstorm a short list of things they might see or do during the day, then make a similar list for night. List student responses under the appropriate headings. Have each student fold a piece of construction paper in half, and copy the word *day* on one side and *night* on the other. Have them illustrate things they see or do during the day and night on the appropriate sides of the papers.

Name _____   Date _____

Listen as your teacher tells you which objects to color.

Fluency Activities
for *Goodnight Moon*

Pre-reading Activity: Tell students that this book is a great bedtime story. Ask students how a reader should sound when reading a bedtime story (relaxed, quiet, sleepy, etc.). Let students share how their parents sound when they talk to them as they are putting them to bed or singing them lullabies. Ask students if you should read this story in a loud, excited voice or a quiet, relaxed voice. Demonstrate both voices as you ask, then let students choose the correct voice and demonstrate chorally. Tell students to listen to how your voice gets softer towards the end of the story.

During-reading Activity: Ask each student to bring in a stuffed animal, doll, etc. Have them read the story to their stuffed animals in a way that will help their animals "fall asleep." You may wish to provide a few extra toys so that every student will have one. To increase the sleepy feeling, have students chorally read this as they prepare for rest period (if your school encourages rest time during the day). After the reading is finished, turn down the lights and let each student put his toy to "bed" by covering it with a piece of cloth, doll blanket, tissue, or paper towel.

Post-reading Activity: Use the Goodnight Patterns reproducible (page 45) to reread the story. Enlarge the patterns if desired, and cut them out, or trace the patterns on flannel or felt to create pieces that will stick to a flannel board. Set up a flannel board in a center and provide copies of *Goodnight Moon*. If you are using paper patterns, attach hook-and-loop tape to the backs of the patterns, and place them on the flannel board. If no flannel board is available, attach a large sheet of paper to a traditional (magnetic) chalkboard, and attach the pieces with small magnets. Read the story aloud as students place the pieces on the board as they are mentioned. Then, let a student read the story while another student finds the appropriate pieces for each page and attaches them to the board. For a more elaborate alternative, collect doll-sized versions of some of the objects in the story, and let students put a bedroom together inside of a large box to make a diorama.

Use these patterns with the fluency post-reading activity (page 44).

Goodnight Moon Patterns

Comprehension Activities
for *Goodnight Moon*

Pre-reading Activity: Tell students that this book is about a bunny who is getting ready for bed. Ask each student to share how she gets ready for bed by illustrating and/or writing the steps in the first column of the We Get Ready for Bed reproducible (page 47). Have students put aside the reproducibles until later, but tell them to keep their responses in mind as you read, to see if the bunny does any of the same things they do. After reading the story, have each student fill in the things that the bunny did to get ready for bed in the second column of the reproducible. Then, discuss the similarities and differences as a class, and let students share any unique bedtime rituals.

During-reading Activity: Discussion is an important part of reading comprehension. Pause throughout the reading to ask and discuss questions such as, "Who are the characters in the story? What is the bunny getting ready to do? What are some things that the bunny is saying good night to? What time of day is it in the book? How do you know? Why do you think the illustrator uses dark colors and shadows? Why do you think the bunny says good night to everything before he goes to sleep? Where do you think the bunny got his red balloon? Do you think the bunny fell asleep at the end? Why or why not?" Make sure that each student has a chance to respond to a question, if possible.

Post-reading Activity: Help students interact with the story by relating it to their lives, and also help them identify and repeat story patterns in the book by having them write or dictate a *Good Morning Sun* version. Discuss what kinds of things the bunny might see in the morning (sun, blue sky, clouds, breakfast, school bus, etc.). Brainstorm a list of things to say good morning to and list them on the board or on a piece of chart paper. Assign each student one item from the list. Have students write about and illustrate their items. Let each student present his good morning page to the class, then bind the pages to create a class book entitled *Good Morning Sun*. Incorporate reading the class book into the morning routine to start the school day, or just before rest period to prepare students for quiet time.

We Get Ready for Bed

comprehension reproducible for
Goodnight Moon

Name_____ Date _____

Things Bunny does to get ready for bed:

Things I do to get ready for bed:

Green Eggs and Ham

By Dr. Seuss (Random House, 1960)

This well-known book tells the story of "Sam-I-am" who doesn't give up until his friend tries (and loves) green eggs and ham. This book is an excellent tool for teaching basic reading concepts such as rhyming patterns, phonics rules, and fluency due to its highly rhythmic and fun-to-read text. Additionally, the book has an excellent life lesson: don't be afraid to try new things!

Related books: These are some of the easier books by this favorite author: *The Foot Book* (Random House, 1968); *Great Day for Up* (Random House, 1974); *Hop on Pop* (Random House, 1963); *One Fish Two Fish Red Fish Blue Fish* (Random House, 1960); *There's a Wocket in My Pocket!* (Random House, 1974)

Phonemic Awareness Activities
for *Green Eggs and Ham*

Pre-reading Activity: Ask students if they eat eggs. Write *eggs* on the board. Ask students if they have ever eaten green eggs and write *green* in front of *eggs*. Explain that the letter e makes a different sound in each word, and have students identify the long /e/ sound in *green*, and the short /e/ sound in *eggs*. Help each student notice the difference in his mouth/lip/tongue placement when saying each letter sound. Point out how one character in the book is tall and Sam is short. Let students use their listening skills to identify the long and short /e/ sounds by standing like the tall character if they hear a long /e/ word or squatting like Sam if they hear a short /e/ word. Some possible story words to use are *them, eat, see, tree, be, let,* and *me*. Be sure to stress the /e/ sound in each word, especially if the phoneme is in the middle.

During-reading Activity: Say the book's title and have students repeat it. Ask what sound they first hear in the word *green* (/g/). Have students say other words that begin with the /g/ sound. Repeat the word *green*, stressing the /r/ sound after the /g/. Ask students what sound they hear after the /g/ (/r/). Have students list words that start with the /r/ sound. Point out that the /g/ and /r/ together make the /gr/ sound, which is called a consonant blend. Have students make the /gr/ sound. Give each student a green crayon. Tell students to hold up their green crayons and make a "grrr" sound each time they hear a word from the book with the gr blend.

Post-reading Activity: After students know the story, work on rhymes. Give each student a copy of the Rhyme Time reproducible (page 49). Review the names of the pictures (bee, coat, socks, jar, chain, park). Have students color and cut out the picture cards. Reread the story, pausing at appropriate places, and have students hold up picture cards that can replace rhyming words from the book. For example, as you read "Not in a box. Not with a _____." (*Green Eggs and Ham*, page 24) students should hold up the socks to finish the sentence.

Name_____   Date_____

Color and cut out the pictures. When your teacher reads a word that rhymes with a picture, hold up the card with that picture.

Phonics Activities

for *Green Eggs and Ham*

Pre-reading Activity: This activity provides students with phonics practice and exposes them to words that they will hear frequently in the story. Tell students that the main character does not want to eat something because he thinks he will not like it. Ask students to talk about foods they like and dislike. Then, ask if they like cereal. Provide alphabet-shaped cereal and tell students that they will use alphabet-shaped cereal to "write" words from the story by listening to the phonemes you say. Slowly pronounce the first phoneme in a word ("h-h-h-h"). Ask students to think of which letter would make that sound and find it in their bowls of cereal. Repeat with the next phoneme ("a-a-a-a"), then the last phoneme ("m-m-m-m"). Then, ask students to sound out the word they created with you. They should say "h-h-h-a-a-a-m-m-m." Ask, "What word do those phonemes make? How did you spell *ham*?" Next, list *ham* on the board as one of the words to find in the book. Repeat with other simple phoneme words from the book such as *am, Sam, and, or, car, not, be, tree, box,* and *fox*.

During-reading Activity: Point out that Dr. Seuss used many of the same words in his many different books. Tell students that sometimes many different words can be built using the same letters. Enlarge and cut out the letters on the Word Builder reproducible (page 51). Attach magnets or tape to the backs of the letters so that they will stick to the board or display the letters in a pocket chart. Display the letters b, o, and x to demonstrate how to build the word *box*. Then, provide students with copies of the reproducible, and have them cut out the letters and build the following story words: *fox, ham, am, Sam, green, eggs, tree, me, be, see, train, rain*. Challenge students to work in groups to discover how many other words they can build with the letter cards.

Post-reading Activity: This activity will give students an opportunity to use what they have learned about invented and real spelling, sounding out phonemes, graphemes, the alphabet, blends, etc. Discuss the problem in the story. (The character did not want to try green eggs and ham because he thought he would not like them.) Discuss the ending of the story. (He tried green eggs and ham and liked them a lot.) Ask students to think of something they have eaten that they first thought they would not like. Consider sharing a personal story from your childhood. Then, have students think about foods they did not want to eat, but tried. Direct students to draw pictures of themselves eating the foods. When students are finished, ask a volunteer to name the food he tried. Repeat the food name and encourage students to help you spell the word. Then, provide assistance for that student to write the name of his food on the board. When that student returns to his seat, allow time for him to copy the name of the food as a title and draw a picture of himself eating the food. When all of the food names have been spelled, combine the illustrations into a class book called *Our New Foods*.

Name _____ Date _____

Cut out the letter cards. Use the letters to make different words.

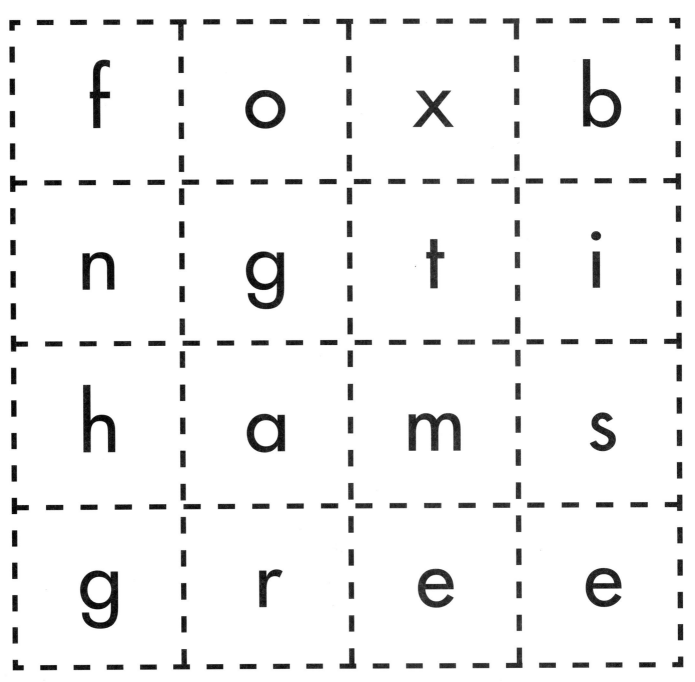

f	o	x	b
n	g	t	i
h	a	m	s
g	r	e	e

Vocabulary Activities
for *Green Eggs and Ham*

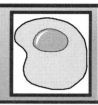

Pre-reading Activity: Before reading the book to students, help them practice "reading" words out of context by teaching words that are often repeated in the book. Tell students that you will give them clues about some words from the book, and have them try to guess what the words are. When they guess a word correctly, list it on a piece of chart paper. For example, say, "The first vocabulary word is a food. You usually have these for breakfast and you can eat them scrambled or hard-boiled." When a student guesses correctly, write the word *eggs* on the chart and give that student a sticky note. Have her draw eggs on the note, then stick it to the chart. Continue with the following words: *ham, house, mouse, box, fox, car, tree, train, dark, rain, goat, boat.* When the chart is completed, have students "read" the words back to you. As you read the story aloud, show the text and have students find the vocabulary words in the story. Revisit the chart often, and challenge students to read the words out of order, use them in sentences, etc. To assess whether students have learned the vocabulary, remove the illustrations and have students read the words without visual clues.

During-reading Activity: Explain that *sight words* are words that readers recognize and can read immediately. Sight words are also called *high-frequency words* because they frequently appear in reading material. Tell students that Dr. Seuss often used high-frequency words, or sight words, in his books. By repeating these words often, he helped children learn these words. List the following words on index cards: *I, am, that, do, not, and, or, with, in, a, are,* and *you.* Repeat some of the words or select more high-frequency words so that there is one card for each student. Show each word card to the class, read the word, and have students repeat it. Then, give the word card to a student. Repeat until all word cards are distributed. Next, read the story aloud and have students hold up their word cards when they see and hear their sight words.

Post-reading Activity: Discuss with students why they thought the character was reluctant to try green eggs and ham. Encourage students to speculate as to why the eggs and ham were green. Ask what colors eggs and ham usually are. Then, ask students if they would try green eggs and ham. After students respond, announce that they will have the opportunity to do just that! With parents' permission, add green food coloring to sliced ham and scrambled eggs warmed in your school's kitchen. Allow students to taste the green eggs and ham. Then, have students name other colors and give examples of other foods that are those colors. Give each student a copy of the Color Words reproducible (page 53) and crayons in corresponding colors. Have each student draw one food with each crayon. For example, a student could draw a banana with a yellow crayon, broccoli with a green crayon, etc. To help each student learn the words, cover each word on his page and have him say or write the words while looking at the pictures.

Name_____   Date _____

In the blank section below, use the correct crayon to draw a different food that matches each color. Cover the words. Name the color of each picture.

yellow   green   red

brown   blue   orange

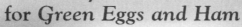

Pre-reading Activity: Tell students that the book *Green Eggs and Ham* is about Sam, who is trying to convince another character to eat something, even though the character keeps saying "no." Ask students how they would feel if someone asked them something, they answered no, and the person insisted. Have students role-play scenarios such as, a mom keeps asking her child to eat something he really doesn't want to eat; a classmate keeps asking if she can keep the new pencil she borrowed; etc. Encourage students to role play with expression. Ask students how their voices would sound if they had to keep saying no over and over to the same question. Ask how their voices would sound if they were trying really hard to convince someone to do something. Explain that in order to help the reader "hear" these strong emotions in the book, the author has repeated some words, used exclamation points, and has written some words in all uppercase letters. Show students examples of these from the book. Have each student write the name of a least favorite food on a copy of the I Said No! reproducible (page 55) to demonstrate and practice reading fluently using such clues. If you want the class to read the same words, make a transparency from the reproducible so that students can read together, and choose a food for the students. Then, tell students to listen for expressive reading while you read the book and to look for clues you discussed, such as question marks, exclamation points, uppercase letters, etc. (Note: If students use irregular plurals, such as meat or spinach, help them adjust the words *these* and *are* on the reproducible.)

During-reading Activity: Due to the rhythm, rhyme, and familiarity of this book, students will want to join you in reading parts of *Green Eggs and Ham* aloud. Encourage them to practice fluency by pointing to the class when you want students to join in chorally or finish a sentence individually. For example, most students will chime in with "I do not like green eggs and ham. I do not like them, Sam-I-am." For this specific pair of sentences, you may want to make a funny gesture, such as holding your nose or making a face, when it is students' turn to read the part of the finicky character.

Post-reading Activity: Because of the silliness, rhyming pattern, and repetitive words, students will want to read *Green Eggs and Ham* independently (and will probably never get tired of hearing it!). Record yourself reading the book fluently and with great rhythm and expression (or provide a professionally-recorded tape). Prepare a listening center where students can go one or a few at a time to listen to the story. Encourage students to follow along and join in when they know the words. Encourage students to listen to the book several times and notice how much better they can read the book the more they hear it read fluently on tape.

I Said No!
fluency reproducible for
Green Eggs and Ham

Name _____ Date _____

Write the name of your least favorite food in the blanks. Use the same food in each blank. Read the page aloud.

Do you like _____?

Oh, no, I do not like _____! I do not like _____ ONE BIT!

Try these _____. They are yummy, yummy, yummy.

No! No! No! _____ are NOT yummy.

These _____ are VERY, VERY yummy.

I do not want _____. _____ are NOT yummy! NO!

Comprehension Activities
for *Green Eggs and Ham*

Pre-reading Activity: Read the title of the story to students and tell them that the book's main character does not want to try green eggs and ham because he doesn't think he will like them. Ask students to predict if he will or will not eat the green eggs and ham. Take a class vote and record the number of students who think he will eat green eggs and ham and those who think he won't. Tell students to keep these predictions in mind while you read the story. Then, ask students if they would eat green eggs and ham. Have them explain why or why not. Have students write and illustrate themselves eating or not eating the green eggs and ham. Provide a sentence format on the board such as *I will/will not try green eggs and ham because* _____. and let students write or dictate their answers. Divide a bulletin board in half and title the halves "We will try green eggs and ham," and "We will not try green eggs and ham." Display the papers on the bulletin board. To extend this activity, surprise students with the vocabulary post-reading activity (page 52).

During-reading Activity: Have students monitor the main character's changing attitude toward green eggs and ham by filling in the beginning, middle, and ending of the story. Give each student a sheet of construction paper. Have him fold it to make three horizontal rows. Write the words *Beginning, Middle,* and *Ending* on the board at the tops of the rows. Have students copy what you have written. After you have read the first few pages of the story, pause and instruct each student to illustrate what happened in the *Beginning* row. Continue reading and pause about two-thirds of the way through the story. Instruct each student to illustrate what has happened in the middle of the story in the *Middle* row. Then, finish reading the book, and instruct each student to illustrate what happened at the end in the *Ending* row. Divide a bulletin board into three sections by lining it with different colors of paper. Label the sections *Beginning, Middle,* and *Ending*. Fold one-third of students' papers so that only the beginning sections are showing. Display these in the *Beginning* section. Repeat for middle and ending sections. Title the bulletin board *Green Eggs and Ham from Start to Finish*.

Post-reading Activity: Copy the Taste-Test Parent Letter (page 57) for students to take home several days before this activity. Tell students that many books teach lessons. Ask what they think the character in the book learned after he tried green eggs and ham and discovered he liked them. Let students share what they learned from this book (to try new things, to not say they don't like something unless they try it, to be persistent like Sam, etc.). Discuss how these lessons can be applied or used in real life. Tell students that they will have the opportunity to try several things and learn if they like them or not. A few days before the activity, send home the Taste-Test Parent Letter (page 57) to recruit parent volunteers to help with the taste test and provide some of the foods. On taste-test day, let each student try a small amount of some of the foods. Help each student keep a record to indicate whether she likes the new foods. Post the class results on a bulletin board. As an alternate activity, modify the parent letter to have each student try one new food at home. For sharing time, let each student talk about trying her new food. Point out if any students tried the same foods. Discuss the results.

Taste-Test Parent Letter
comprehension reproducible for
Green Eggs and Ham

Student's Name _____ Date _____

Dear Parents/Guardians,

We are currently reading *Green Eggs and Ham* by Dr. Seuss. In the book, Sam tries to convince another character to try green eggs and ham. Although the character insists throughout the book that he absolutely does not like green eggs and ham, he finally gives in. After trying green eggs and ham, he is surprised to find he loves them! The lesson is don't be afraid to try new things. We will discuss this lesson in class and how it applies not only to food, but to life in general (meeting new people, trying new activities, going to new places, etc.).

To bring this lesson "to life" we will have a taste test. Students will try different foods and decide whether they like them. If you can help by donating an "interesting" food item for the taste test, please fill out the section below and bring the item in on _____. Either way, please fill out the information below and return this form with your child so that he/she can participate. If you have any questions, please do not hesitate to contact me. Thank you in advance for your support!

Sincerely,

_____

Green Eggs and Ham Taste Test Permission Form

_____
Child's Name

Can your child participate in the taste test? Yes   No

Can you bring something in for the taste test? Yes   No

If yes, what food will you bring? 1st choice _____ 2nd choice _____

Please list any food allergies your child has. _____

_____   _____
Parent/Guardian Signature   Date

If You Give a Moose a Muffin
by Laura Joffe Numeroff
(Laura Geringer, 1991)

This silly book is a circular story of what happens when a boy gives a moose a muffin. The text is simple enough that young readers will easily begin to read along as they become familiar with the story.

Related books: *If You Give a Mouse a Cookie* by Laura Joffe Numeroff (Laura Geringer, 1985); *If You Give a Pig a Pancake* by Laura Joffe Numeroff (Laura Geringer, 1998)

Phonemic Awareness Activities
for *If You Give a Moose a Muffin*

Pre-reading activity: Read the title to students. Ask them to identify the initial phoneme in the words *moose* and *muffin*. Have students make the /m/ sound. Explain that the book is about what happens when a boy gives a moose a muffin. Challenge students to think of other things the boy might give the moose that also begin with the /m/ phoneme. Have each student draw one of the /m/ phoneme items on the a copy of the moose pattern (page 59). When students have finished, call on them to share their /m/ ideas. Write the letter m in the middle of a bulletin board or piece of chart paper. If a student's picture begins with the letter m, have him attach his moose pattern to the bulletin board or chart paper. If a student selects a picture that does not start with m but contains the letter, then underline the m in the word and have her attach the pattern to the bulletin board or chart paper.

During-reading Activity: Review the short /i/ sound by finding short /i/ words in the title (*if, give, muffin*). Have students indicate that they hear that sound during the read-aloud by calling out the short /i/ sound. When students call out the short /i/ sound, pause and have students say the word in which they heard the phoneme. Reread that word and confirm or correct whether it has the short /i/ phoneme.

Post-reading Activity: Review and identify the short /a/ phoneme. Reread page 17 of the book on which the moose tries to cover his antlers as they stick out from behind a couch. Write *antlers* on the board and identify the initial short /a/ phoneme. Tell students to try to think of other ways for the moose to cover his antlers. Copy two antler patterns (page 59). Program one antler *short /a/*. Turn over the other antler and label the back *not short /a/*. Copy both antlers on heavy paper for each student to cut out. Staple the antlers to sentence strips, then staple the ends of the strips to make headbands. Have students wear their antlers and work in pairs to think of other things that might cover the moose's antlers, such as blankets, shirts, hats, etc. Let students draw and cut out the objects, then glue short /a/ objects on the short /a/ antler. Have them glue other objects on the not short /a/ antler. Have students read their object names aloud and listen to each other's words for the short /a/ sound.

Moose and Antler Patterns

phonemic awareness reproducible for
If You Give a Moose a Muffin

Name_____ Date _____

On the moose pattern, draw and color something you would like to feed the moose that begins with the letter m. Cut out the moose pattern. Save the antler pattern for later. Your teacher will tell you what to do.

Pre-reading Activity: The word *moose* gives students a perfect opportunity to practice recognizing the /oo/ sound as in moose. Have students say the word *moose*, exaggerating the /oo/ sound. Ask volunteers to brainstorm other words that have the /oo/ sound and are spelled with oo. Examples might be *tool, boot, roof,* and *root* (depending on regional pronunciation), *school, drool, pool, boo, moo, fool, loot, scoot, toot, shoot,* and *goose*. Plan a time to celebrate the /oo/ sound during the school day. Get students involved by encouraging them to call out "Mmmoooooosssse!" every time they hear someone use the /oo/ sound. Write the words on the board, separating the words that are spelled with the letters oo, and those that are spelled differently (such as fruit, juice, etc.). Make sure you designate a time for students to stop making the sound. At the end of the school day, let each student individually brainstorm and write a list of /oo/ words she has heard throughout the day.

During-reading Activity: Tell students that when they are reading there will be many times when they come to a word they do not know. Ask students what they might do when this happens and write their ideas on the board. Explain that a good reader has many strategies or tricks he can use when he doesn't know a word. For example, a good trick is to look at the pictures for a clue. If the pictures don't help, have students try sounding out the first letter of the word and ask themselves what would make sense there. Tell students that sometimes by using these tricks together, they can easily figure out words they don't know. Demonstrate this while reading the story. For example, read, "When he puts the sweater on, he'll notice one of the _____ . . . ." (*If You Give a Moose a Muffin*, page 9). Think aloud, "I don't know this word. When I look at the picture for clues, I see the moose is putting on a sweater. I see something falling off the sweater. I think it is a button. The moose is looking at this button, so it might be important in the reading. Let me go back to the word I didn't know and use those clues to sound it out. The word in the sentence starts with the letter b. I know the word must start with the /b/ sound. *Button* starts with the /b/ sound. Maybe the word is button. Let me read the sentence again and see if that makes sense. When he puts the sweater on, he'll notice one of the b-b-buttons is loose (*If You Give a Moose a Muffin*, page 9). Yes, that makes sense because the button is falling off the sweater in the picture. Also, the word looks like it could be *button* because it starts with the /b/ sound, and I see two t's in the middle and an n at the end. Button. Yes, that's it." During reading, give students opportunities to practice using this strategy by pausing at words that offer good picture clues such as *door, sewing, cardboard, paints, antlers, sheet,* and *yard.*

Post-reading Activity: If possible, share *If You Give a Pig a Pancake*, also by Laura Joffe Numeroff (Laura Geringer, 1998). Ask students what they notice about the names of the animals and the foods fed to them in both books. Help students name the animals and the foods that have the same beginning letters and sounds. Explain that when words in a phrase start with the same beginning sound, it is called *alliteration*. Brainstorm other animals and write them on the board. Have students think of foods that can be given to the animals that start with the same letters as the animal names. Then, have each student complete a copy of the "Animalliteration" reproducible (page 61) by choosing an animal and a food that begin with the same letter. Have students use invented spelling to complete the sentences, then illustrate them and share with the class. Bind the pages into a class book titled *Animal Appetites*.

"Animalliteration"
phonics reproducible for
If You Give a Moose a Muffin

Name_____ Date _____

Write the name of an animal in the first blank. Write the name of a food in the second blank. The name of the animal and the name of the food should start with the same letter or letters. In the third blank, write something else your animal would want that also begins with the same letter. Draw a picture about your sentence. Then, cut out your work.

If you give a _____ a _____ ,

it will want a _____ to go with it.

Vocabulary Activities
for *If You Give a Moose a Muffin*

Pre-reading Activity: It is important for students to learn that, in addition to looking them up in the dictionary, unknown vocabulary words can often be defined by using context clues and/or picture clues. Write the story words *scenery* and *antlers* on the board and read them aloud. Before showing students the book or the cover, ask them what they think these words mean. Write their guesses on a piece of chart paper. Then, explain that it is easier to figure out a word when it is not "all by itself," but is in a sentence or a book with clues from the story words (or *context*) and the pictures. Tell students to look for the words *scenery* and *antlers* as you read the story. Pause at appropriate pages and help students figure out the meanings of the words by pointing out picture and text clues. For example, say, "It says the moose wanted to make scenery. I see in the picture that he is painting something on a piece of cardboard on the wall. I also know that he needs this for his puppet show. When I turn the page, I see a picture of the moose putting on a puppet show behind the couch, like it's a stage, and the cardboard drawings are behind him. What do you think *scenery* is, then?" Then, review the guesses on the chart paper and compare them to the new definitions. Repeat this for *antlers* and other new words.

During-reading Activity: Prior to this activity, copy the Muffin Compounds reproducible (page 63), cut out the muffin halves, and shuffle them. Write the word *homemade* on the board. Ask students how many words they "see" inside of the word *homemade*. Ask students what they think it means when something is homemade. Ask them how the two words (*home* and *made*) help them know the meaning of *homemade*. Tell students that when two words are put together to make a new word it is called a *compound* word and that there are many compound words in the story. Ask students to brainstorm other compound words. Then, show the muffin half cards to students and read each word, having students repeat. Randomly give one muffin half card to each student. As you read, have students look for their words in the story. When a compound word appears in the text, have the two students that have the parts of the compound word stand up, read their words, and put them together to make the compound from the story.

Post-reading Activity: Expose students to contractions, since there is at least one on almost every page of the book. List the contractions *he'll, you'll, he's, they're,* and *it'll* on the board, and have students find them in the book. Read some of the sentences that contain these words. (Point out that *he'll* shows up on almost every page.) Tell students that each of these words is a *contraction*, or a short way of saying two words. Reread the first sentence containing the contraction *he'll*. Replace the contraction with *he will*. Explain that *he'll* means the same thing, but it is shorter. Write the words *he will* next to the contraction. Ask students what they notice about the contraction *he'll* and the words *he will*. (Some of the letters are missing in the contraction, and it has an apostrophe.) Tell students that the "little thing" that looks like an upside-down comma in the contraction is an *apostrophe* and it takes the place of missing letters. To make this concept more concrete, give an index card programmed with the word *he* to a student. Give four other students cards with the letters w, i, l, and l. Have students stand together so the class can read *he will*. Give another student a card with an apostrophe and ask students holding the w and i cards to sit down. Have the student with the apostrophe card stand in his place and have the class read *he'll*. Repeat with other contractions from the story.

Muffin Compounds

vocabulary reproducible for
If You Give a Moose a Muffin

Name_____ Date _____

Use with the vocabulary during-reading activity (page 63). Have students cut out and match the muffins to make compound words.

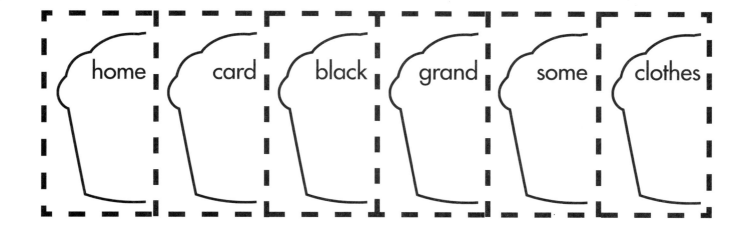

home   card   black   grand   some   clothes

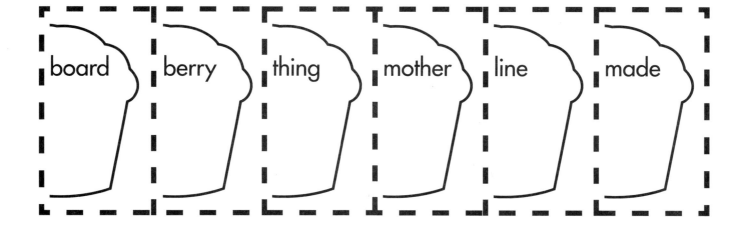

board   berry   thing   mother   line   made

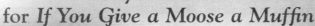
Fluency Activities
for *If You Give a Moose a Muffin*

Pre-reading Activity: Remind students that part of being a fluent reader is knowing which parts of a story should be read more loudly or softly. Tell students that sometimes an author will use all uppercase letters to indicate that something should be read in a loud, shouting voice. Ask students why a character in a book might use a loud shouting voice (angry, calling someone far away, etc.). Tell students that the author of this book used one word in all uppercase letters to show that it should be read in a loud voice. Write the word *BOO!* on the board. Ask students to read the word and guess why the author chose to write that word in all uppercase letters and why there is an exclamation point after it. Tell students to look for the word when you read the story and to notice how your voice changes when you reach the word.

During-reading Activity: Have students make moose puppets using old socks (like the moose did in the book) or moose masks out of paper plates. Provide each student with a copy of The Moose Is Talking! reproducible (page 65), and let them echo read the text several times. When you read each page on which the moose is asking for something, have students read the corresponding moose "dialogue" on the reproducible, using their puppets. For example, when you read, ". . . he'll want some jam to go with it" (*If You Give a Moose a Muffin*, page 9), students will read, "May I have some jam to go with it?" Encourage students to use "moose voices" and actions with their puppets, and proper expression. When students are confident that their reading is fluent, pair them to repeat the exercise. Students will enjoy hearing each other's "moose voices."

Post-reading Activity: This book's text formatting makes it a good tool to practice fluency. Turn to the beginning of the book where it says that the moose would want another, and another, etc. Reread those sentences and point out how they are broken up into chunks to give the reader an idea of the rhythm. Ask, "Do you see how 'And another. And another.' (*If You Give a Moose a Muffin*, pages 5-6) is written together? Did you hear how I read the two words together, then took a break, and read the next two words together? I did that because the author split up the words that way so I'd read them that way." Have students practice reading the sentences on these pages fluently by echo reading or choral reading. Then, turn to the end of the book where it says "And chances are . . . if you give him the jam, he'll want a muffin to go with it." (*If You Give a Moose a Muffin*, page 28-29). Point out to students how the words *And chances are* are written alone on one page so that they will be read together. Show students the ellipse and tell them that those are used to tell the reader to let her voice trail off. Model this for students by reading this page aloud. Then, have students imitate by chorally or echo reading the page.

The Moose Is Talking!

fluency reproducible for

If You Give a Moose a Muffin

Read the following sentences with your moose puppet as your teacher reads the story.

1. May I have some jam to go with it?

2. May I have another?

3. May I have another?

4. May I have another?

5. Can you make more?

6. May I go with you?

7. May I borrow a sweater?

8. May I have a needle and thread?

9. May I have some old socks?

10. May I put on a puppet show?

11. May I have some cardboard and paints?

12. Will you help me make the scenery?

13. May I have something to cover up my antlers?

14. BOO!

15. May I have some soap?

16. May I hang up the sheet to dry?

17. May I have some jam?

18. May I have a muffin to go with it?

Comprehension Activities

for *If You Give a Moose a Muffin*

Pre-reading Activity: Read the title to students and show them the cover illustrations. Explain that this is a book about what happens when a boy gives a moose a muffin. Have students list their predictions about what will happen if you give a moose a muffin. This can be done in a number of ways. Let students give oral responses as you list them on a piece of chart paper. Have students draw their predictions and share with the class. Allow students to use invented spelling to write their own predictions. Or, let the class brainstorm predictions and agree on one prediction to write on the board. Revisit predictions after reading the book.

During-reading Activity: Tell students that this book depicts a "chain of events." Explain that a chain of events is when one thing makes something else happen, then that makes something else happen, and so on. Explain that these actions are called *causes and effects*. Give each student a copy of the Chain of Events reproducible (page 67) to complete as you read the story. Show students that the first two boxes have already been partially filled in. Pause at each event in the story to give students time to draw the events in the boxes. If students need more space, encourage them to use the back of the reproducible.

Post-reading Activity: Give an example of a cause-and-effect chain of events such as, "If you stay up late to watch television, then you will wake up late the next morning. If you are late, you won't have time to eat breakfast. If you don't eat breakfast, you will be so hungry at school that you are in a bad mood, so you will have an argument with a friend. If you argue with a friend, you will want to forget about it, so to forget about it, you stay up late to watch television." Have students sit in a circle on the floor. Begin by naming the first event in the book ("If you give a moose a muffin . . ."). Then, ask a student to tell about the next event. This could be something like, ". . . he'll ask for a blueberry one next." Then, ask the next student to say the next event, such as, "He'll go outside to look for blueberry bushes," and so on, until each student has had a turn. As students respond, either record the activity on tape and then transfer it to writing, or write their responses as they go. Turn the responses into a class book by having each student copy and illustrate his response. Title the book *Our Class Version of If You Give a Moose a Muffin*.

Chain of Events

comprehension reproducible for
If You Give a Moose a Muffin

Name_____ Date _____

Listen as your teacher reads *If You Give a Moose a Muffin*. As each event happens, draw the event in the next box. Finish on the back if you need more room.

The moose gets a muffin and asks for some jam to go with it.	The moose gets some jam to go with his muffin and asks for _____.

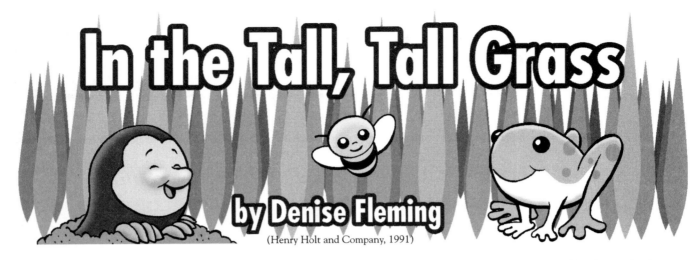

In the Tall, Tall Grass

by Denise Fleming

(Henry Holt and Company, 1991)

This simple rhyming book describes all of the things a caterpillar hears and sees as he walks through the tall, tall grass. This book is an excellent tool for teaching rhymes, word families, and simple phonics.

Related books: *In the Small, Small Pond* by Denise Fleming (Henry Holt and Company, 1998); *Lunch* by Denise Fleming (Henry Holt and Company, 1996); *Where Once There Was a Wood* by Denise Fleming (Henry Holt and Company, 2000)

Phonemic Awareness Activities
for *In the Tall, Tall Grass*

Pre-reading Activity: Tell students that they will be reading a book called *In the Tall, Tall Grass*. Ask students what sound they hear at the beginning of the word *tall*. Tell students that they will be hunters and have them pretend to walk through tall, tall grass in search of objects with the same beginning sound as the word *tall*. Have students demonstrate how they might move if they were hunters walking through tall, tall grass. Give students a few minutes to "hunt" around the classroom, to find /t/ objects. Then, direct them back to their seats and have them draw the objects they found whose names begin with the /t/ phoneme. Have "hunters" share their discoveries with the class.

During-reading Activity: Review the concept of rhyming words. Use words in the book's title to form rhyming words. For example, ask students, "What rhymes with *in*?" After the review, as you read the story aloud, pause and give students an opportunity to identify the rhyming story words within the story. Record their answers on a piece of chart paper, and repeat the activity with the words *the*, *tall*, and *grass*.

Post-reading Activity: Explain that many words in the story have the same endings, so they make up word families. Select some words from the book to reread aloud. Have students identify the beginnings and endings (or *onsets* and *rimes*). For example, say, "What phoneme do you hear at the beginning of *tug*?" Students should answer "/t/." Respond with, "Yes, *tug* begins with /t/. What does the word *tug* become when I take away the /t/?" Students should answer "ug." Respond with, "That's right. If you take away /t/ from *tug*, you have ug." Then, change some phonemes in the word. Have students show you if the word ends with ug and is part of the word family by giving a thumbs-up or thumbs-down. Say words like *bug*, *snug*, *rug*, etc., then say, "Luck." Students should indicate with a thumbs down. Continue with other word families from the book such as unch, ip, um, ap, ide, um, ap, atch, urry, ip, op, oop, and ight. Use the Word Families reproducible (page 69) as an extension or assessment.

Name_____ Date _____

Cut out the picture cards and the word cards. Match each picture to its name. Then, put the cards with the op ending in one pile, the cards with the ap ending in a second pile, and the cards with the ug ending in a third pile.

| mop | cap | rug |
| bug | map | stop |

Phonics Activities
for *In the Tall, Tall Grass*

Pre-reading Activity: Read the book title to students and tell them that the story is about a caterpillar who munches his lunch. Ask students what they think a caterpillar might munch for lunch. Accept any responses. Briefly let students crawl around the classroom while pretending to be caterpillars munching their lunches. Reveal to students that the caterpillar in the story eats tall grass for his lunch. Write the word *tall* on an index card, tear off the t, and tell students that the caterpillar has munched the letter t for lunch. Ask students what word is left after the caterpillar has munched the t (*all*). Let students pretend to be caterpillars by "munching" different letters to create new words. On index cards, write words from the story, such as *lunch, dart, sip, drum,* etc. Make one card per student. Randomly pass out word cards and have each student read his word, "munch" off the first letter of the word, and then read the new word or word ending. After students have finished, take turns calling on each student to show and read her original word, share what letter she munched, and read her new word to the class. The new words can be nonsense words, as long as students can show they are able to delete the first letter.

During-reading Activity: This activity can be done at a center or as a class, depending on the amount of materials available. Prior to this activity, have the class help you gather twigs, tall grasses, and other natural materials (if you do not have access to these, make tall "grass" from construction paper or paper streamers). Explain that students will practice "writing" words from the story with the natural materials. Give each student some of the gathered materials. Read the story and pause at each page. Reread one or more words from the page that you would like students to "write" with the materials. Have students form the shapes of the letters with the natural materials. This activity can be tailored to suit your students' specific needs and levels. For example, if you want to review rhyming words, have students "write" the rhyming words from each page with their materials, and then think of other rhyming words to "write." After students have had practice with writing, let them glue their words to construction paper. Display them on a bulletin board.

Post-reading Activity: Teach students to form new words using the onsets and rimes from the story. First, review some of the words in the story with the same rimes (endings) such as *crunch, munch, lunch.* Provide students with copies of the Animal Rhymes reproducible (page 71). Next, have each student look at the letters and blends on the reproducible. Help students write the letters and blends in the correct boxes to form words from the story as well as new words. Tell students to look at the animal and insect shapes on the worksheet to remind themselves of what animals do in the story. If this activity is too advanced for some students, turn this into a whole-class or small group activity. Enlarge the reproducible to poster size and cut off the letters at the bottom of the page. Write each letter or blend from the reproducible on an index card. Find the action words in the text with students. Ask students where to place the index cards on the poster to make the words.

Animal Rhymes

phonics reproducible for
In the Tall, Tall Grass

Name_____ Date _____

Read the letters at the bottom of the page. Write the letters in the correct blanks to make new words. Use the animal and insect pictures as clues.

|unch

|unch

|ip

|ip

|um

|um

|oop

|oop

|op

|op

|ide

|ide

fl	gl	sl	h	sw	s
l	str	h	cr	d	m

Vocabulary Activities
for *In the Tall, Tall Grass*

Pre-reading Activity: Tell students that they will be reading a story about some animals and insects and what they do in the tall grass. Before they read the story, it is important that they know the vocabulary word for each animal or insect in the book. To reinforce this meaning, have students pretend to be those animals and insects. Give each student a card from the We Are Animals reproducible (page 73) and have him color it (picture names are hummingbird, bird, ant, snake, beetle, mole, frog, rabbit, and bat). Pin or tape the animal or insect pattern to the student's shirt (or punch a hole in each pattern and string it on a length of yarn to make a necklace). Then, have students move around the room acting like their animals and insects. Encourage students to think about the noises their animals and insects make, how they might move, what they might eat, etc. After a few minutes, have students return to their seats. Have one group at a time (all of the bees, for example) say their animal or insect name, what it does, how it moves, etc. After all of the animals and insects have been discussed, tell students to look for their animals in the book and see if the behaviors they identified match those listed in the book.

During-reading Activity: Tell students that a *noun* is a word that names a person, place, or thing. Ask students to give examples of words that name people and list responses on the board. Then, have students give examples of words that name places and add these words to list. Repeat for things. As you read, have students identify nouns in the book by raising their hands when they hear you read them. When a student raises his hand, ask him which word on the page is a noun and whether it is a person, place, or thing. (Give students a hint: all nouns in the book will be things.) Instead of having students raise their hands, you may want them to hold up their patterns from the pre-reading activity. Have students hold up the animal or insect cutouts when they hear you read the corresponding noun. This will be easier for students because the cards held up will be the nouns in most cases.

Post-reading Activity: After reading the text, review the action that each animal or insect does. Reread the action words on the pages and have students act them out. For example, have students do a gliding motion with their arms or bodies for "snakes glide." Tell students that words that show action are called *verbs*. Give each student a sheet of construction paper and help her fold it horizontally into four sections. Then, help her fold the paper vertically into three sections, to create 12 sections when she opens her paper. Finally, have each student write a different verb from the story in each section and illustrate the animal doing this action. If 12 words are too many for students, let them fold their papers into fewer sections.

We Are Animals

vocabulary reproducible for
In the Tall, Tall Grass

Name_____ Date _____

Copy, cut out, and distribute the cards randomly to students. Use with the vocabulary pre-reading activity (page 72).

Fluency Activities
for *In the Tall, Tall Grass*

Pre-reading Activity: Tell students that good, fluent readers look carefully at the way words are written and at punctuation. Prior to reading the story, flip through the pages and point out how the text is written. Have students notice the commas between the "sound words" on most of the left-hand pages, and the way the "animal and action words" are grouped together on most of the right-hand pages with no commas. Tell students that commas are signals that tell readers they have to pause (or take a little breath) while reading. Explain that the words on most of the right-hand pages are grouped together, so they should be read together. Read an excerpt from the book, and ask students to notice the pause at the comma and the "chunking" of the two animal and action words.

During-reading Activity: This is an excellent book for practicing echo reading because the text is simple and rhythmic. Additionally, the text can be read aloud with emphasis on certain words, such as speeding up "skitter, scurry, beetles hurry" (*In the Tall, Tall Grass*, pages 17-18), or stressing the /s/ in the action words for the snake. Students can imitate the moods of the phrases as well as the sounds of the words. Tell students that they will echo, or repeat, the reading after you. Practice with the title. Then, pause every two pages and have students echo read. Discuss why you read certain words differently.

Post-reading Activity: Reread the book while clapping the rhythm. Because the text does not overwhelm students, the rhythms are simple to clap while still providing enough rhythm to make clapping effective. Once students have demonstrated the ability to clap with the text, pass out copies of the Rhythms of the Grass reproducible (page 75). Read the poem once with the class, and point out how the pictures provide clues to help them read the text. Then, divide students into small groups or pairs and have them practice reading the poem fluently while clapping the rhythm. Let volunteers "present" to the class. If students seem to enjoy this activity, assign some to chant the poem and others to play instruments along with the poem.

Rhythms of the Grass
fluency reproducible for
In the Tall, Tall Grass

Name_____ Date _____

Read the poem below. Clap the rhythm as you read. Color the picture.

In the grass, the caterpillars crunch,

The snakes slide,

The bees buzz,

and the rabbits hide!

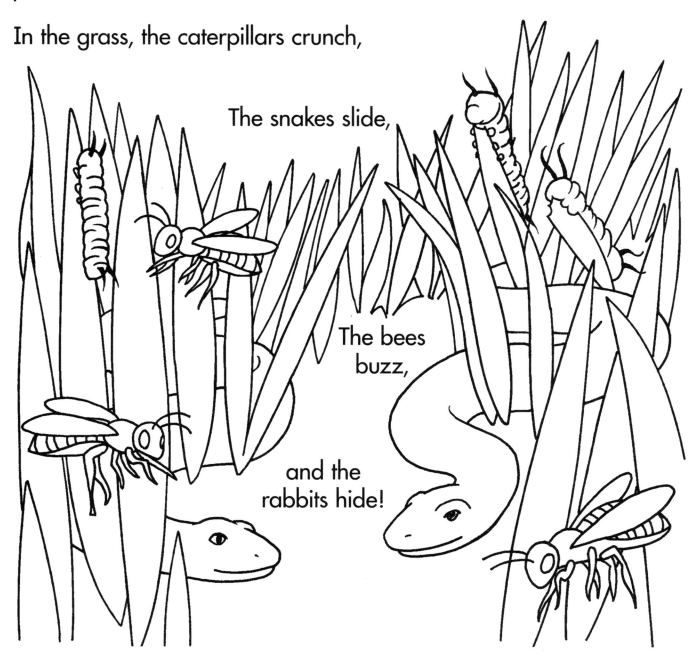

Comprehension Activities
for *In the Tall, Tall Grass*

Pre-reading Activity: Show the book cover to students and read the title. Ask students to predict what kinds of things the boy on the cover might find in the tall, tall grass. Encourage students to think of things they have seen in the grass. List predictions on a piece of chart paper, and tell students that as you read, you will put a check next to predictions that appear in the book. You may also wish to take students outside to examine a patch of grass. Let students make predictions based on what they see in the grass during the exploration.

During-reading Activity: Tell students that good readers think while they read to make sure that they understand what they read. Have students check their own understanding as you read the story aloud. Give students a strip of green construction paper (about 3" x 11"). Show students how to make the paper look like tall grass by snipping slits in one long edge of the strip without cutting all the way through. Then, give each student an 8" x 11" piece of yellow construction paper background (similar to the illustrations in the book) and have her glue the green grass along the bottom edge of the yellow paper. Tell students that as you read the book, they should draw the animals and insects that you mention. This will help them practice checking themselves while they are reading to make sure they are understanding. Read the book and pause after every two pages to give students a few minutes to draw the animals or insects that appear in the book. Encourage them to illustrate the animals and insects doing whatever the book says they are doing. Tell students not to worry about coloring their animals yet so that you can continue reading the book at a moderate pace. After the book is finished, allow students to add color and details to their drawings. Then, display the illustrations on a bulletin board titled "Checking Our Comprehension in the Tall, Tall Grass."

Post-reading Activity: After reading the book, go on a nature walk. Have students take notepads and pencils to record things they see while walking through a grassy area. Encourage students to crawl on the grass and get low to the ground the way the boy in the book did. Have students list (or draw) what they see on the nature walk. After returning to the classroom, compile a class version of the book based on students' notes. Write students' observations on a piece of chart paper, following the pattern on the A Walk in the Tall, Tall Grass reproducible (page 77). For example, a student might say, "In the tall, tall grass, ants march. In the tall, tall grass mosquitoes buzz." Give each student a copy of the reproducible, and have him select a sentence he would like to write and illustrate. Encourage each student to illustrate an entire page, following the illustration patterns from the book. Then, compile the pages into a class book titled "In Our Tall, Tall Grass." If there is not a grassy area nearby, let students use any safe, outdoor area where they can closely observe. Retitle the class book to reflect the new setting.

A Walk in the Tall, Tall Grass

comprehension reproducible for
In the Tall, Tall Grass

Name_____ Date _____

Write your sentence on the lines. Illustrate your sentence.

In the _____

_____.

Leo the Late Bloomer
by Robert Kraus

(Windmill Books, 1971)

Leo is a young tiger who can't do anything right. His father compares him to others and asks what's wrong with him. Leo's mother insists that he is just a "late bloomer." Throughout the book, Leo's dad pretends not to watch for "signs of blooming." Finally one day, Leo suddenly "blooms" and can read, write, and do other things. The book sends a relevant message to students who may also feel like late bloomers. The text is simple, natural, and lends itself to teaching phonics, vocabulary, suffixes, and idioms.

Related books: *The Carrot Seed* by Ruth Krauss (HarperCollins, 1988); *I Like Me!* by Nancy L. Carlson (Viking Press, 1988); *Thank You, Mr. Falker* by Patricia Polacco (Philomel Books, 1998)

Phonemic Awareness Activities
for *Leo the Late Bloomer*

Pre-reading Activity: Read the title aloud. Ask what phoneme students hear three times (/l/). Have them say the /l/ sound. Point out how their tongues touch the roofs of their mouths. Identify the letter that makes the /l/ sound in the title. As you say a list of words from the story (*Leo, late, bloomer, sloppy, blooming, still, bloomed, neatly, also, whole*), intersperse them with other story words that do not have the /l/ sound. When students identify a word with the /l/ phoneme, have them repeat the word, stressing the /l/ phoneme. Tell students to listen for words with the /l/ sound as you read the story.

During-reading Activity: Note that in this story, Leo can't do many things his friends can do, like talk. Skip ahead and read the line, "And, he never said a word" (*Leo the Late Bloomer*, page 7). Explain that just like Leo was silent, some letters, like the letter *l*, can be silent, too. Review the sound that the letter *l* usually makes. Have each student look at the text as you read, and signal the letter by raising her left hand and forming an uppercase L with her pointer finger and thumb. When students signal an L, stop and reread the word. Ask students to decide if the l is silent or if it makes its regular sound. (Students should see that the words *could* and *couldn't* appear in the text.)

Post-reading Activity: Continue work with the letter l. Provide each student with a copy of the Letter L reproducible (page 79). Have him place the "shh-ing" and shouting tiger cutouts on a table as "headers," then shuffle the word cards. As you read the words on the word cards, have students repeat each word to decide if it contains a silent l. If a word does contain a silent l, have each student put that word card on his desk under the "shh-ing tiger." If a word does not contain a silent l, have him put that word card under the shouting tiger cutout. Circulate around the room and review each word in order to give students immediate feedback and clear up any confusion. Use the tiger cutouts with other cards to study other silent letters.

Name_____ Date _____

Cut out the shh-ing tiger, the shouting tiger, and the word cards. Place the tigers next to each other. Place each card with a word that has a silent l under the shh-ing tiger. Under the shouting tiger, place each word with an l that makes the l sound.

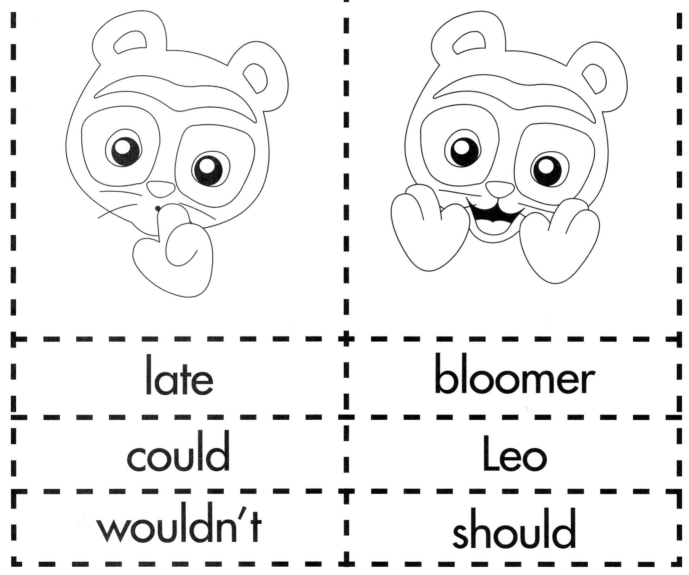

late	bloomer
could	Leo
wouldn't	should

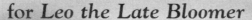

Phonics Activities
for *Leo the Late Bloomer*

Pre-reading Activity: Tell students that *Leo the Late Bloomer* is about a little tiger who can't do many of the things his friends can do, like read and write. Prepare a class chart with two columns. Label one column *Things We Can Do Already* and the other *Things We Can't Do Yet*. Tell students to help you fill in the chart by giving ideas and by helping you spell words. Ask students to name activities or skills for each column. As you write, ask them to help you spell the words. For example, say, "OK, we can kick a ball. How would I write the word *kick*? Sound out the word. What is the first sound?" Students should answer "/k/." Write a k on the chart. Move to the next sound in the word, showing students the letter-sound correspondences in each word. Explain that not all sounds correspond directly to their letters. For example, the /k/ sounds in the word *kick* are represented by both k and ck. Continue the exercise by letting students help spell the simple words they name for the *Things We Can't Do Yet* side of the chart.

During-reading Activity: While reading the book, pause when it says, "He also spoke. And it wasn't just a word. It was a whole sentence" (*Leo the Late Bloomer*, page 26). Ask students what the difference is between a word and a sentence. Explain or review that a *word* is made up of letters, while a *sentence* is made up of words and expresses a complete idea. After reading the sentence that Leo said ("I made it!"), ask students how many words were in his one sentence, then help students count and name the letters in each word. Repeat this with a few pages until students display understanding of the concepts.

Post-reading Activity: This activity extends the phonemic awareness post-reading activity (page 78). Move from silent l to other silent letters. Look in the book at the word *late*. Show students how adding e to the end of a word makes the /a/ say its name. Review with other words from the book, such as *write* and *made*. After students are able to identify the long vowel sound in vowel/consonant/silent e words from the book, tell students to build words with the "magic e." Provide students with copies of the Magic E reproducible (page 81) and have them cut out the letter cards. Create a teacher set of letter cards and model the activity for students by building a word using a consonant/vowel/consonant pattern (such as *cap*). Have students read the word and identify the vowel sound made by the middle letter. Then, have students add the "magic e" to the end of the word (*cape*), read the word, and identify the new vowel sound. Let students build *can/cane, cap/cape, pin/pine, kit/kite, cut/cute, pan/pane, rat/rate, cub/cube, not/note,* and *tub/tube*. For students who are not yet ready to grasp this concept, work with small groups to manipulate the cards, but focus on the sounds and how they change.

Name_____ Date _____

Cut out the letters. Use the letters to make words. Add the silent e to each word to make a new word.

c	a	n
p	i	u
t	e	r
o	k	b

Vocabulary Activities
for *Leo the Late Bloomer*

Pre-reading Activity: Because the word *bloom* is used so often throughout the book, it is critical that students understand this concept prior to reading the story. A few days before this activity, ask each student to bring in a baby picture. Provide a seed, a small plant, and a flower. Ask students to compare the seed, the plant, and the flower. Guide students toward understanding that the fully grown flower has bloomed. Then, have students share their baby pictures and compare them to how they look now. Tell students that they, too, have "bloomed" like the flower. Write the word *bloom* on the board. Have students read it and explain what it means (to grow and flourish). Read the book title to students and tell them that it is about a tiger named Leo who "blooms" late. Have students predict what *bloom* means in this context.

During-reading Activity: Students will love the other animals in this book. As you reach the page on which the animals are writing their names, pause and look at the different animals. Ask students to describe each animal. (They will probably need help with *plover.*) Distribute copies of the Leo's Friends reproducible (page 83) and have students cut out the animals. Read each fact below without saying the name of the animal and let students identify which animal it tells about by holding up their matching cards. Copy some of the facts below onto index cards and place them with the patterns from the reproducible in a center for students to quiz themselves.

- This bird has immobile eyes and a large head. Its fluffy feathers make its flight almost silent. It spits out pellets of bones and other things it cannot digest. (owl)
- This large animal can be African or Indian, has a trunk and a tail, and can weigh as much as 16,500 pounds. Most of them can grow tusks. (elephant)
- This animal can be poisonous. It moves by contracting its muscles. When it grows, it sheds its scaly skin. (snake)
- This bird lives all over the world except where there is ice. It likes to wade in water. Some kinds of this bird clean crocodiles' teeth. (plover)
- This animal floats on water so it can see and breathe and catch animals to eat. It lays eggs and looks similar to an alligator. (crocodile)

Post-reading Activity: Prior to this activity, give five index cards to each student. After reading the story, have students find all of the different "versions" (bloom as noun and verb, bloomed, blooming, bloomer, etc.) of the vocabulary word *bloom*. List them on the board. Ask students what is the same in all of the words on the list (*bloom*). Have each student write one letter in the word *bloom* on each card. Tell each student to "build" the word *bloom* by putting the letter cards in order. Then, pass out two more cards to each student and have them label those cards *e* and *r.* Ask students what the word *bloom* becomes when they add these letters to the word (*bloomer*). Repeat with letter cards for i, n, g, and e, d. Ask students which letters did not change as they removed and added new endings to the word (*bloom*). Tell them that *bloom* is the base word, and the endings are called *suffixes.* If students seem to understand the concept, practice adding suffixes to other words.

Leo's Friends
vocabulary reproducible for
Leo the Late Bloomer

Name_____ Date _____

Cut out the animals. Listen as your teacher reads about each animal. When you think you know which animal your teacher is reading about, hold up the matching picture.

Fluency Activities
for *Leo the Late Bloomer*

Pre-reading Activity: The following activity will not only provide students with practice in fluency, it will also serve as an excellent "opener" for the book's theme. Send home copies of the Fluency Parent Letter reproducible (page 85). After parents fill in the requested information, have students practice reading the sentences until they are able to read them fluently. Then, have each student return the bottom half of the form and take turns reading her sentences to the class. Use the readings to open a discussion on how everyone "blooms" or grows at different rates, like Leo in the story.

During-reading Activity: Point out to students how there are four "voices" speaking in the story: the narrator who tells the story, Leo's mother, Leo's father, and Leo (at the very end of the book). Tell students that when characters talk in a story it is called *dialogue*, and that today they will be reading the story according to these "voices." Tell them that you will read the narrator's parts, the boys will read Leo's father's parts, the girls will read Leo's mother's parts, and the whole class will read Leo's part at the end. If necessary, you can read the father's and mother's parts with students (chorally) or read them first and have students echo read. Encourage students to read fluently and with expression. They may even want to incorporate character voices!

Post-reading Activity: This book lends itself well to readers' theater because all of the parts are short and fairly simple, which makes it easy for students to learn their parts. Divide students into small, heterogeneous groups. In each group, assign narrator's parts to one, two, or three of the most proficient readers. Assign the parts as follows: the mother's part to the next-most proficient readers, the father to the next, and Leo to the least-proficient readers. Tell students reading the part of Leo that they are very important, since the entire book is about the character of Leo. Give groups time to rehearse. Encourage them to include actions, facial expressions, voice intonations, and movements in their "plays." Consider having students make props and/or masks as well. When groups are ready, have them perform the book for the class. Provide specific praise for fluent readers such as, "Great expression when you read the mom's part!" or "I really like the way you made Leo's voice sound when he finally spoke." To help less proficient readers, let them read more difficult parts as they become more familiar with the book. If you prefer to do this in larger groups or as a whole-class activity, assign students to act out the parts of Leo's friends. Instruct them to make appropriate animal movements and noises, use character voices, and think about their facial expressions as they read.

Fluency Parent Letter
fluency reproducible for
Leo the Late Bloomer

Child's Name _____ Date _____

Dear Parents/Guardians,

We will be reading the book *Leo the Late Bloomer* by Robert Kraus. This is the story of Leo, a tiger who can't do any of the things his friends do: read, write, draw, eat neatly, or speak. Leo's father is worried, but Leo's mother insists that Leo is just "a late bloomer." Leo does indeed "bloom" at the end!

We will use this book to discuss growth and how different people learn to do things at different times. This activity will also help your child develop fluency, an important reading skill. You can help in the following ways:
* 	Fill in the blanks below in handwriting that your child will be able to read.
* 	Talk to your child about this activity and the sentences below.
* 	Read the sentences aloud a few times so that your child hears what a fluent reader sounds like.
* 	Listen to your child practice reading the sentences several times, until he/she can do so as fluently as possible for him/her.
* 	Praise your child's efforts!
* 	Cut along the dotted line and have your child bring in the form ready to read it aloud to the class on _____ .

Thank you!

Sincerely,

_____

- -

Describe Your "Blooming"

Child's Name _____

I learned how to walk when I was _____ old.

I learned how to talk when I was _____ old.

I drew my first picture when I was _____ old.

My first word was _____ .

Comprehension Activities
for *Leo the Late Bloomer*

Pre-reading Activity: Help students understand the idiomatic definition of being a "late bloomer." Even though idioms are a fairly abstract concept for young students, with some guidance they will understand and enjoy them! As you read, pause after the sentence "A watched bloomer doesn't bloom" (*Leo the Late Bloomer*, page 14). Discuss with students what they think Leo's mom meant by that. Ask them if they think watching a flower (or a person) really discourages blooming. Tell students that this expression is an *idiom*. Ask students if they have ever heard someone say, "A watched pot never boils." Discuss what that might really mean. Ask, "Does watching a pot keep the water inside from boiling? Will it boil immediately when someone looks away?" Share and discuss other common idioms such as, It's raining cats and dogs; I'm so hungry I could eat a horse; I have butterflies in my stomach; She put her foot in her mouth; Lunch was on the house; The new car cost an arm and a leg; Michael caught a cold; Alexandra lost her temper; My mom has a green thumb; etc. Make copies of the Idiom Pictures reproducible (page 87). Write a different idiom on each student's paper, and have her illustrate what the idiom says literally. Then, have different students explain what the idioms actually mean. Model this first to ensure understanding, or do as a whole-class activity. Display the finished work on a bulletin board titled "It's Just an Expression . . . ."

During-reading Activity: As you read the story, pause at appropriate places and discuss some of the following questions: "What does Mom mean when she says he's just a late bloomer? How do the illustrations help the reader tell how Mom feels and how Dad feels? Was Leo's dad really not watching? Why do you think Leo's dad really did watch? How do you think Leo felt when he finally bloomed? How does Dad look on the last page? Why do you think Leo's sentence on the last page was 'I made it!'?"

Post-reading Activity: Show students comic strips and point out the speech balloons and thought bubbles. Discuss how the bubbles show what a character is thinking. Discuss how Leo and his parents might have been feeling and what they might have been thinking. Create a web of ideas for each character's feelings on the board so that students have something to refer to during the activity. Model how to write from each character's perspective. Draw and cut out a set of thought balloons. As you reread the book, ask students at different points what they think some of the characters are thinking. Write responses in the thought bubbles. Number them on the backs. After you and students finish a set of thought bubbles, place the bubbles in a center along with a copy of the book. Let students take turns reading the book and matching thought bubbles to the correct pages in the book.

Idiom Pictures

comprehension reproducible for
Leo the Late Bloomer

Name_____   Date _____

Your teacher will write an idiom on the lines. Draw what the idiom says. Then, talk with your teacher about what the idiom really means.

_____

_____

Miss Bindergarten Gets Ready for Kindergarten

by Joseph Slate

(Dutton Children's Books, 1996)

This rhyming alphabet book depicts Miss Bindergarten and her students as they get ready for the first day of kindergarten. This book lends itself to teaching rhyme awareness, which is an important skill to learn in the early stages of phonemic development. It is also an alphabet book, so it can be used for simple initial phoneme development and to reinforce learning the alphabet.

Related books: *Miss Bindergarten Celebrates the 100th Day of Kindergarten* by Joseph Slate (Dutton, 1998); *Miss Bindergarten Stays Home from Kindergarten* by Joseph Slate (Dutton, 2000); *Miss Bindergarten Takes a Field Trip with Kindergarten* by Joseph Slate (Dutton, 2001)

Phonemic Awareness Activities
for *Miss Bindergarten Gets Ready for Kindergarten*

Pre-reading Activity: Explain that *Miss Bindergarten Gets Ready for Kindergarten* is about characters who are getting ready for the first day of kindergarten. Show the first few pages of the book and point out how it is an alphabet book because each page uses a letter from the alphabet in alphabetical order. Review each letter name and phoneme, and ask students whose names (first or last) begin with that letter to stand up. For example, say, "A. If your name starts with the letter a, stand up. Alicia. A-a-alicia. The character whose name starts with a is Adam. A-a-adam. A-a-alicia." Continue with all of the letters.

During-reading Activity: Review the concept of rhyming words before beginning to read the story. Then, let students identify the rhyming words on each page as you read. Begin reading aloud and pause after "Adam Krupp wakes up." (*Miss Bindergarten Gets Ready for Kindergarten*, page 1). Ask students which two words rhymed. Let a volunteer list the pair on the board. Continue reading and pause for each character to let the class identify and list the rhyming words. After finding all of the rhyming words, revisit the rhyming pairs. Have students read each pair and verbally add at least one rhyming word. For example, "Krupp, up, cup."

Post-reading Activity: Have students practice initial phoneme identification by matching the picture cards on copies of the ABC Phonemes reproducible (page 89) to characters' names. Copy the reproducible and randomly distribute picture cards to students. Briefly review the names of the pictures. Reread each character's name from the book. When you read the first name of the character, have the student who has the picture card with the picture that begins with the same phoneme stand up. Repeat the character's name and the picture name ("Adam, apple.").

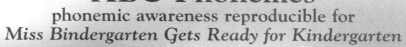

ABC Phonemes

phonemic awareness reproducible for
Miss Bindergarten Gets Ready for Kindergarten

Use the letter cards with the phonemic awareness post-reading activity (page 88).

Phonics Activities
for *Miss Bindergarten Gets Ready for Kindergarten*

Pre-reading Activity: This activity gives students an opportunity to practice phonics in an authentic writing activity, and also helps develop prior knowledge for reading the book later. Read the title of the book aloud and ask students to brainstorm things they do each morning to get ready for kindergarten. Use the word *kindergarten* as an example for how to sound out and write a word. Start with the /k/ sound and write a k on the board. Then, sound out the short /i/ sound and add the letter i. Continue sounding the phonemes and writing the corresponding letters and combinations on the board. Have students sound out the letters with you. To extend the activity, have each student write a simple sentence about getting ready for kindergarten. Model the activity for students by sounding out words, then writing and illustrating your sentence. Have each student write and illustrate his own version using his first and last name and a morning activity. Provide writing assistance by either allowing students to dictate to you, use invented spelling, or copy phrases you have provided on the board from the initial brainstorming session.

During-reading Activity: Write the alphabet on a piece of chart paper or a long piece of bulletin board paper. As you read *Miss Bindergarten Gets Ready for Kindergarten*, pause at each letter and ask students to name different words that start with that letter. As they do this, discuss the connection between letters and sounds. Write each word under the correct letters while comparing letters and sounds again, and draw a simple picture for each word. Repeat for the entire alphabet. Then, have each student complete a copy of the Alphabet Words reproducible (page 91) by selecting one word that begins with each letter, writing it, and illustrating it on a separate piece of paper. Encourage students to keep these lists to refer to for future alphabet activities. Post the alphabet chart in the classroom or add some of the words to a word wall.

Post-reading Activity: Write a class version of *Miss Bindergarten Gets Ready for Kindergarten*. Following the same pattern as the book, rewrite the story on a piece of chart paper or the board using students' names. For example, instead of Adam, substitute student names that begin with A, such as, *Abigail wakes up. Adrian wakes up*, etc. Focus on the initial graphemes instead of the rhymes. Use the original characters' names when you do not have a student whose name begins with that letter. Publish the book by having each student copy her sentence and illustrate the page for her own name. Then, bind the pages together. Read the sentences aloud and take time to discuss how many names you have for each letter, etc. Change Miss Bindergarten's name to your name if you wish to add and illustrate a page of your own.

Alphabet Words

phonics reproducible for
Miss Bindergarten Gets Ready for Kindergarten

Name _____ Date _____

On each line, write a word that begins with the letter.

A a _____   B b _____   C c _____

D d _____   E e _____   F f _____

G g _____   H h _____   I i _____

J j _____   K k _____   L l _____

M m _____   N n _____   O o _____

P p _____   Q q _____   R r _____

S s _____   T t _____   U u _____

V v _____   W w _____   X x _____

Y y _____   Z z _____

_____

Vocabulary Activities

for *Miss Bindergarten Gets Ready for Kindergarten*

Pre-reading Activity: Point out the word *ready* in the title and explain that this is a book about how a teacher and her students get ready for the first day of kindergarten. Write the word *ready* on a piece of chart paper. Ask students, "What are some places you have to get ready for? How do you get ready for something? What did you do to get ready for school today? How would you get ready for a party? How do we get ready for lunch? How do you get ready for bed? What are some synonyms for *ready*?" Brainstorm ideas with students. Write students' ideas on a web or list.

During-reading Activity: This activity is an excellent introduction to verbs. As you read *Miss Bindergarten Gets Ready for Kindergarten*, pause for each character and ask students what word in the sentence is the action that the character is doing to get ready for kindergarten. For example, read aloud, "Christopher Beaker finds his sneaker." (*Miss Bindergarten Gets Ready for Kindergarten*, page 2) Ask, "What does Christopher Beaker do?" Students should answer, "Finds." Continue reading as students identify the action word on each character page. Tell students that these words are *verbs*. Reread the story and select a different volunteer to act out the verb on each page. See the post-reading activity for an extension and assessment.

Post-reading Activity: To review verbs, play action charades after the during-reading activity. Whisper an action word in a student's ear and have him act it out for the class to guess. Once students are used to the activity, make it more competitive by forming teams. Let each student take a turn acting out a verb as his team guesses. If the team guesses correctly, give that team a point. If the team does not guess correctly, then allow the other team to guess. For a more challenging variation of the game, let students suggest words for you to act out as the class guesses. (This is more challenging because students have to think of the verbs themselves and you have to be a good actor!) Then, use the Action Words reproducible (page 93) to assess or provide further practice with verbs.

First-Rate Reading™ Grade K • CD-0068 • © Carson-Dellosa

Action Words

vocabulary reproducible for
Miss Bindergarten Gets Ready for Kindergarten

Name _____ Date _____

Color the pictures that show action. On the back of this page, draw a picture that shows action.

Fluency Activities
for *Miss Bindergarten Gets Ready for Kindergarten*

Pre-reading Activity: Explain that characters in the book are getting ready for kindergarten. Ask students what kinds of things a kindergartner learns how to do. Tell students that one thing kindergartners begin to learn is how to be fluent readers. Explain that to be fluent, readers must sound "good" reading aloud. Tell students they should sound natural, like when they speak; they should not read too fast or too slowly; they should take little breaths and pause when they are supposed to, they should use their fingers or other objects to follow along (track print) as they read. Give an example of each of these actions as you prepare to read the book aloud. Tell students to listen carefully and watch for those things when you read the story because one of the best ways to become a more fluent reader is to listen to other fluent readers.

During-reading Activity: Point out to students how certain words should be grouped or "chunked" together as you read aloud. For example, ask, "Do you hear how I group together the words 'Henry Fetter' and 'fights his sweater'? (*Miss Bindergarten Gets Ready for Kindergarten*, page 9). Wouldn't it sound strange if I had read it 'Henry' [pause] 'Fetter fights' [pause] 'his sweater'?" Since the rhythmic pattern of the alphabet pages is broken up occasionally with the line "Miss Bindergarten gets ready for kindergarten," demonstrate chunking with this sentence too.

Post-reading Activity: Have students (either as a whole class or in groups) choral read aloud with you. This is especially effective with a book such as *Miss Bindergarten Gets Ready for Kindergarten* due to its rhythm and rhyme. After students are familiar with the book, meet with students one-on-one to assess fluency development. For this particular book, pay special attention to "chunking" and rhythm. Complete the Fluency Assessment reproducible (page 95) for each student. Consider reassessing after a few weeks, in order to gauge students' progress.

First-Rate Reading™ Grade K • CD-0068 • © Carson-Dellosa

Fluency Assessment

fluency reproducible for
Miss Bindergarten Gets Ready for Kindergarten

Student's Name _____ Date _____

Circle Yes, No, or Partial to monitor each student's fluency development and progress with *Miss Bindergarten Gets Ready for Kindergarten.*

1. Student can chorally read a section of the book with you.
    Yes No Partial

2. Student can point to text appropriately as you read it aloud.
    Yes No Partial

3. When asked, student can identify spaces between words.
    Yes No Partial

4. Student knows what spaces are for (pause, take a breath, etc.).
    Yes No Partial

Comments: _____

_____

_____

_____

_____

_____

_____

_____

_____

Comprehension Activities
for *Miss Bindergarten Gets Ready for Kindergarten*

Pre-reading Activity: This activity promotes comprehension by establishing prior knowledge as well as helping students make personal connections with the literature. Tell students that *Miss Bindergarten Gets Ready for Kindergarten* is about getting ready for the first day of kindergarten. Invite each student to share how she felt on her first day of kindergarten. Then, have each student compose a journal entry on how she felt that first day. Allow students to use invented spelling, illustrations, dictation, or a combination of these to write how they felt. Finally, let each student preview the pictures to choose one character which represents something he did on the morning of the first day of school.

During-reading Activity: As you read the story, pause to discuss details about the text and illustrations. Ask students to notice what Miss Bindergarten does to get ready for kindergarten. Challenge students to find details such as what her cockatoo does, the notes she sticks around the room, the books she puts on the shelf, the tag sticking out of her dress, etc. Let students comment on whether they do some of the things the characters in the book do to get ready.

Post-reading Activity: Have students compare and contrast the setting of the story to their own kindergarten classroom. Discuss with students how the book takes place in Miss Bindergarten's classroom. Tell them that this is the *setting*, and that every story has a setting. Look through the book and challenge students to look for details in the illustrations. Have students find things in Miss Bindergarten's kindergarten that they have in their classroom and things they do not have in their classroom. (Review the concepts of same and different, if necessary.) Using copies of the Classroom Comparison reproducible (page 97), have students compare and contrast the two kindergarten classrooms. For an extension to this activity, have students use invented spelling, dictation, or copying the words from the board to label pictures of the items.

Classroom Comparison
comprehension reproducible for
Miss Bindergarten Gets Ready for Kindergarten

Name_____ Date _____

Draw a picture of something you see in Miss Bindergarten's kindergarten. Then, write your teacher's name and draw a picture of something you see in your kindergarten.

Miss Bindergarten's kindergarten

M_____'s kindergarten

(Harcourt Brace and Company, 1984)

This predictable book uses rich colors and fine details to tell a cumulative story about a house where everyone is sleeping, until a flea sets off a chain of events, and everyone is suddenly wide-awake!

Related books: *This Is the House That Jack Built* by Pam Adams (Child's Play International, Ltd., 1989); *There Was an Old Lady Who Swallowed a Fly* by Simms Taback (Viking Children's Books, 1997); *Why Mosquitoes Buzz in People's Ears* by Verna Aardema (The Dial Press, 1975); *The Doorbell Rang* by Pat Hutchins (Greenwillow, 1986)

Phonemic Awareness Activities
for *The Napping House*

Pre-reading Activity: Read the title to students and ask them to identify the initial phoneme in the word *napping*. Have students identify other students, friends, or family members whose names begin with /n/. Pronounce these names carefully, focusing on the initial phoneme, then have students call out other words that begin with /n/. Repeat this activity with the /h/ phoneme. Tell students to listen for /n/ and /h/ when you read the book.

During-reading Activity: While reading, continue the pre-reading activity by categorizing words by /n/ and /h/ phonemes. First, say random words that begin with either the /n/ or /h/ phoneme. When students hear each word, have them identify the /n/ sound or /h/ sound immediately. Use "outside voices" if possible. (Students will listen carefully for the opportunity to shout the phonemes.) Provide two index cards for each student. Have him write a letter h on one index card and a letter n on the other. As you read the story again, have students listen for words containing the /n/ or /h/ phoneme. (They will hear *napping* and *house* on each page.) When they hear one, instruct them to hold up the correct letter card. Stop and ask students to name the word they heard with the /n/ or /h/ phoneme. Reread the word to confirm the response and have students identify where in the word the /n/ or /h/ phoneme is located. Enlarge the /N/ and /H/ Phonemes reproducible (page 99) and have students practice.

Post-reading Activity: Slowly pronounce the three phonemes in the word *nap* (/n/, /a/, /p/). Have students repeat them. Repeat the three phonemes while clapping each sound in order to help students hear the three distinct sounds. Have students repeat clapping. Ask students what word is formed when the phonemes are put together. Model by repeating the three phonemes slowly, then blend them together until students "hear" the word. Repeat this process with the word *bed*. Continue the clapping step to assist students in distinguishing between the three phonemes. Practice with other three-phoneme words such as *cat, dog, bed, flea*, etc.

Name_____ Date _____

Cut out the picture cards. Say the name of each picture aloud. Then, place the /n/ cards in one pile and the /h/ cards in another.

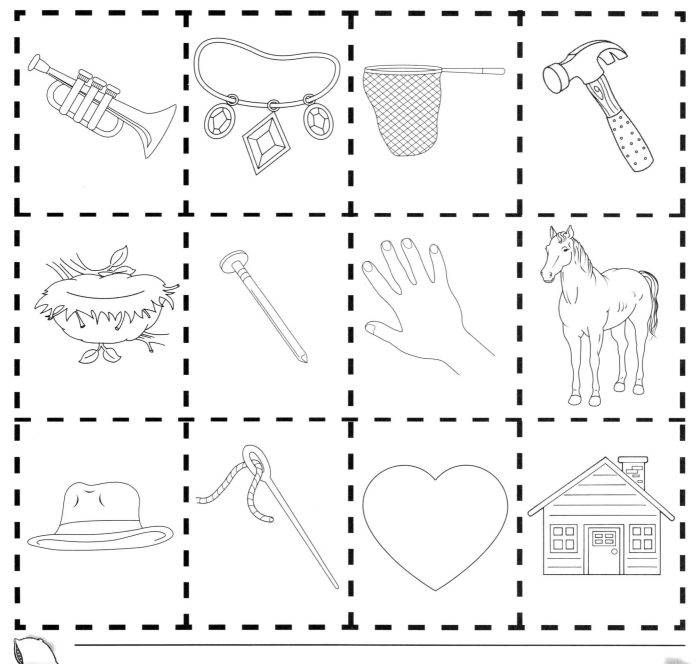

Phonics Activities

for *The Napping House*

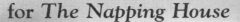re-reading Activity: Students need opportunities to practice phonics in real writing activities. Many students also like to make lists. Give them an opportunity to do both. Write the word *napping* on the board and underline the n. Explain to students that they can make many new words by placing other letters in place of the letter n. Write *_apping* on the board ten times in a list format. Let students take turns replacing the n with different letters. Suggest that they use more than one letter at a time (blends and digraphs) to create words, as well. Then, underline the real words such as *chapping, clapping, flapping, mapping, rapping, sapping, tapping, trapping,* and *zapping.* Circle the nonsense words. Repeat all of the words aloud as a class.

uring-reading Activity: To build on the phonemic awareness activities in which students worked with the /n/ and /h/ phonemes, have students find words containing the letters n and h in newspapers or magazines. Have students highlight or underline the letters n and h in words they find. (Students will feel very grown-up using highlighters!) Help students cut out the words and sort them into two piles or glue them into two collages. Provide copies of the /N/ and /H/ Word Pictures reproducible (page 101). Have students draw and label n and h items they might find in the napping house. Allow students to use invented spelling as long as the initial letter is correct. Brainstorm and demonstrate a few ideas first.

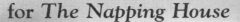ost-reading Activity: This activity builds on the phonemic awareness post-reading activity (page 98). Give students practice building words using graphemes. Provide students with cutout letters, letter tiles, letter blocks, or alphabet-shaped cereal. Slowly pronounce the sounds in the word *nap*. On a desk or table, model how to build the word by placing the correct alphabet letter for each sound. Have students copy this at their desks. Say phonemes for simple words and have students build words by placing letters that represent each phoneme. For example, say "/b/, /e/, /d/." Stretch out each phoneme so that students do not immediately hear the actual word. Have students repeat and place a letter for each phoneme. Then, have students read the words they built. Circulate around the room and give assistance and praise. Have students build other words by focusing on placing each letter as the phoneme is pronounced. Continue to work on basic three-grapheme words such as *cat*. Beware of building three-phoneme words such as *name*, which may confuse students due to the silent e pattern.

/N/ and /H/ Word Pictures

phonics reproducible for
The Napping House

Name_____ Date _____

Draw and label three things you might find in the napping house that begin with the letter n. Then, draw and label three things that you might find in the napping house that begin with the letter h.

n | h

Vocabulary Activities
for *The Napping House*

Pre-reading Activity: To help students comprehend stories, it is helpful to first teach them difficult or important vocabulary. Teach the words *napping* and *cozy*. Ask students what *napping* means. Use questions like, "Have you ever taken a nap? What do you do when you take a nap? What is another word for nap?" Then, ask, "What do you think *cozy* means? What do you think Granny's bed is like if it's cozy? Do you have a favorite spot in your house where you like to snuggle and relax because it's very cozy?" Discuss places, feelings, etc., that are cozy. To reinforce the feeling of the words, turn down the lights when you are discussing the words.

During-reading Activity: Pause while reading to point out the different words the author uses to mean *napping* such as *sleeping, snoring, dreaming*, etc. List them on a piece of chart paper as you encounter them. Tell students that there are many different words that you can use to mean the same thing, and they are called *synonyms*. Have students repeat the word *synonyms* after you. Continue teaching this concept with the post-reading activity below.

Post-reading Activity: Provide and discuss other examples of synonyms, such as *said/spoke, laugh/giggle, shout/yell*, etc. Once students seem to understand the concept, assign them to pairs or small groups. Give each group a word card from the Synonyms reproducible (page 103) and tell students to think of at least one other word that means the same thing as the word on their group's card. Ensure that groups know and understand the words on their cards. Circulate around the room, offering assistance when necessary. After a set amount of time, have students share the words on their cards and synonyms with the class. Challenge the class to come up with additional synonyms for each group's word.

Synonyms
vocabulary reproducible for
The Napping House

Give each group of students one card. Use these with the vocabulary post-reading activity (page 102).

nice	good	pretty	big
woman	man	cold	small
laugh	bad	run	jump
walk	hot	loud	fun

Fluency Activities
for *The Napping House*

Pre-reading Activity: Many students freeze when they are reading aloud and come to an unknown word. Teach "word-attack" reading strategies. Explain to students that sometimes they will come to words they do not know while reading aloud. Ask them to offer suggestions as to what they can do to solve this problem. (Most will immediately suggest, "Ask the teacher/parent/someone.") To guide them towards providing other solutions, ask, "What else can you do? Can you look at the first letter? How does that help you?" Use the Word-Attack Strategies reproducible (page 105) to explain what students can do when they encounter words they do not know in oral reading. Explain that the mouth should remind a reader to sound out difficult words, the rope should remind a reader to skip over a difficult word and keep reading, and the lightbulb should remind a reader to think about the word and guess what it might be. After discussing the reproducible, model the strategies and let students practice in small groups. For example, write the phrase *the slumbering mouse* on the board. Model saying the beginning sound (s), reading the rest of the sentence and going back to the word, guessing what would make sense when all of the other words mean *sleeping*, etc. Provide students with copies of the reproducible to color and keep for reference. Give students other examples on the board to practice in their groups. Create a poster-sized version to display in the classroom. Try to refer to the reproducible at least once during reading so that students can practice with actual text.

During-reading Activity: This activity works particularly well for fluency practice because of the many sequential characters in this book. Reread the story using puppets, stuffed animals, or paper character cutouts. Create a set of character puppets or cards (laminate the cards for durability), and reread the story. Display each character as a visual cue for text. When you are finished with the activity, place the puppets in a center along with a copy of *The Napping House* and let students recreate the story individually.

Post-reading Activity: Students' oral reading is usually better when they read something that they dictated or wrote because their own writing is familiar and personal. Ask a student to tell you a story about a time when she was sleeping and something woke her up. Tell her that her story can be true or pretend. Write the story exactly as the student tells it to you. Then, have the student practice her fluency by reading her story aloud. Provide appropriate praise and feedback, and help her recognize difficult words (students usually have more advanced speaking vocabulary than writing vocabulary). For more practice, assign students to pairs and have them reread their stories to each other.

Name _____   Date _____

Read the word-attack strategies below. Color the pictures. Keep this paper to help you when you come to a word you don't know.

When I don't know a word, this is what I can do.

1. Say the beginning sound, then sound out the rest.

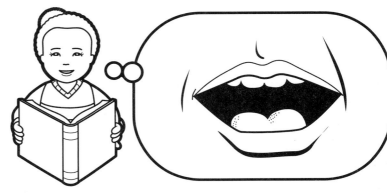

2. Skip it and read on.

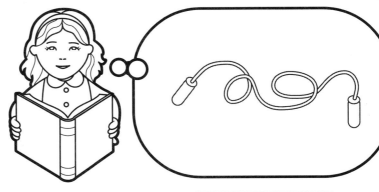

3. Think and guess.

Comprehension Activities
for *The Napping House*

Pre-reading Activity: Introduce cause and effect by lining up a row of standing dominoes and ask students what will happen if you tip over the first one (or use a similar concrete activity). Confirm their predictions by tipping the first domino and watching the rest fall. Discuss that tipping the first one (*cause*) made the rest of the dominoes fall (*effect*). Discuss other examples of cause and effect. Tell students that *The Napping House* is a chain of causes and effects which are all started by a little flea. Have students predict what events a little flea could possibly cause. List students' predictions on the board to revisit later. After reading, have students complete copies of the Cause and Effect reproducible (page 107) and compare the answers to their original predictions.

During-reading Activity: Explain that *details* are little things in text or pictures that help the reader understand the story. Tell students that sometimes details are easy to miss but are very important, and that there are many details in *The Napping House*, especially in the illustrations. Give the example of how all of the story characters are in the illustrations, even from the very beginning, but are hard to notice. Ask students to find all of the characters in the illustrations starting with the second page. Help students find the flea, in particular, on each page. Tell students that the illustrator (who is also the author) added details to the drawings to make it fun to read the story over and over. Challenge students to find other details in the illustrations such as the pillow that falls on the dog's head. Note how the perspective changes as the pile grows; by the end of the story, the reader is "looking" down almost from the ceiling. (This is easy to identify when looking at the changes in the cat bed and water pitcher.) Finally, note how the illustrations' colors change from beginning to end. Choose several details from the story and talk about why the author may have included them.

Post-reading Activity: Tell students that each story has characters and settings (places where and time when the stories happen). Ask students to name the characters in the story and where this story takes place (in Granny's bedroom, in the napping house). Expand the discussion about setting by asking when the story happens, as well (on a rainy afternoon). Ask students, "Might the story have been different if the setting had been different? If it had started as a sunny day, would Granny have been sleeping at all? What if it had been in the middle of the night? Would the characters have woken up to go outside?" Create flap books to explore characters and setting. Give each student a piece of heavy paper. Have her fold her paper in half horizontally, then cut the top flap vertically in the center (perpendicular to the fold). Instruct each student to write *Characters* on one flap and *Setting* on the other. Have each student illustrate some of the characters under the character flap and draw the setting under the other flap. Post the illustrations on a bulletin board titled "Characters and Setting." Let small groups look under the flaps and talk with you about the pictures and what the words *character* and *setting* mean.

Name_____ Date_____

Cut out the events and tape them together in the right order.
Number the events in the order that they happened in the book.
Write each number in its box.

No, David!
By David Shannon

(The Blue Sky Press, 1998)

Little David is always getting into trouble in this Caldecott Honor Book. The text is simple, the illustrations humorous, and the message familiar. This book lends itself to teaching the letter n and its phonemes, and long vowel sounds. Also, it is an excellent tool to develop fluency and discuss a valuable lesson.

Related books: *Olivia* by Ian Falconer (Atheneum, 2000); *David Goes to School* by David Shannon (The Blue Sky Press, 1999); *David Gets in Trouble* by David Shannon (The Blue Sky Press, 2002)

Phonemic Awareness Activities
for *No, David!*

Pre-reading Activity: Explain that as a child, the author wrote a book that showed him doing "bad" things. He wrote "No David!" on each page because they were the only words he could spell. Say the word *no*. Stress the long /o/ sound. Ask students what sound they hear at the end of *no* (long /o/). Give more examples of /o/ words and stress the /o/ phoneme in each (*open, nose, boat*, etc.). Remind students that a long vowel sound makes a letter say its own name. Say the word *David* and stress the long /a/ sound. Have students repeat. Review long /a/ and the other vowels' long sounds. Say several words containing long vowel sounds. Have students indicate which long vowel sound they hear. Enlarge and distribute copies of the Long Vowel Sort reproducible (page 109) for teacher-directed practice.

During-reading Activity: Ask students to say "no." Repeat it with students while stressing the /n/. Ask what sound students hear at the beginning of the word. Tell them to notice what their mouths, lips, and tongues do as they make the /n/ sound. Find objects (and people) that begin with the /n/. Ask students what the word *no* would be if the /n/ was changed to /b/. Say, "/b/, /o/" and stress the /b/. Read the story aloud, changing the initial phoneme in *no* throughout the book. Have students repeat the new words.

Post-reading Activity: Give students a concrete way to isolate and count phonemes. Say "no" with a distinct pause between the phonemes ("/n/—/o/"). Ask students to repeat and count how many sounds they say. Clap once for each sound to distinguish between the phonemes. Repeat the word faster each time until students can identify the phonemes as the word *no*. Give each student two different colored blocks (or squares of colored paper). Explain that the blocks represent the number of sounds they hear. Say, "/b/, /o/" and place a block as you pronounce each phoneme. Have each student repeat the phonemes and place one block for each sound as he says it. Have students raise their hands when they know the word. Repeat the phonemes with a shorter pause in between if needed. Continue with other two-phoneme words such as *day, bee, eat*, etc.

Long Vowel Sort

phonemic awareness reproducible for
No, David!

Name_____ Date _____

Cut out the cards. Sort the pictures by long vowel sounds. Use the letter cards to label the piles.

Phonics Activities
for *No, David!*

Pre-reading Activity: Read the title to students. Ask students how the word *no* is spelled. Guide students through sounding out the word and writing it on the board. Ask students to name other words that begin with the letter n and "help" you spell them on the board, as well. Assign students to pairs or small groups (preferably of mixed ability so that more advanced students can assist others in their groups). Have them brainstorm, write, and illustrate words that begin with the letter n on pieces of poster board. Then, let the groups present the words to the class. To make the activity more interesting, give prizes for different categories such as longest word, most phonemes, most syllables, shortest word, word with the most n's, etc.

During-reading Activity: This activity works well with *No, David!* because there are very few words on each page. Copy each word from the book onto an index card. Prior to reading, shuffle the cards, read them aloud, and distribute them randomly to students. Explain that students will "rewrite" the book as you read aloud by building the story with the word cards, because it will help them to sound out the words slowly, look for the beginning letters, and know whether they have the matching word. Display an empty pocket chart (or attach magnets or tape to the backs of the cards). As you read each word, emphasize the initial phoneme and pause so that students can hear the phoneme and look for the grapheme. Encourage students who have matching words (or initial matching graphemes) to raise their hands. In some cases, more than one student will have the same word. Choose one student's card each time. Have each student come to the pocket chart and place his word in order, to match the text from the page you just read. As you proceed through the read-aloud, the story will build on the pocket chart. Display the pocket chart and word cards in a center along with copies of the book. Let pairs of students practice reading and building the story.

Post-reading Activity: Write sentences or words from the story on sentence strips, leaving out some letters. For example, write _o, David! or Don't __ay with your foo_! The graphemes you remove will depend on your students' levels and areas in which they would benefit from review or practice. For example, if students have just learned to identify final consonants, remove only final consonants. Display the sentence strips in a pocket chart or on the board. Help students to read them and find the missing graphemes. Have students refer to the text for help if necessary. Once the missing graphemes are identified, choose one student to write each missing letter in the blank or on a sticky note to complete each word. Use the Missing Graphemes reproducible (page 111) to assess students' progress or provide further practice.

Name _____ Date _____

Circle the missing letter above each word. Then, write the letters you circled on the lines.

b   m   g   d   e   c

__oy   __ood   b__d

s   t   q   d   a   p

__oys   ba__   b__ll

Vocabulary Activities
for *No, David!*

re-reading Activity: This activity helps students think about language and also prepares them to recognize the different ways Mom says no in the book. Read the title to students. Ask students what it means when someone says, "No." Ask students to share times their parents have said no. Tell students that in this book, David's mom spends a lot of time saying no—almost on every single page! Tell students that they will notice that David's mom doesn't always use the word *no* to mean no. Ask students how else a person can say no such as *uh-uh, nope, I don't think so, never, absolutely not,* shaking his head from side to side, etc.

uring-reading Activity: Ask students to find new words in the book or words that they may have heard before but are not sure what they mean. Possible vocabulary to discuss includes *enough, instant,* and *settle.* Guide students to use context clues as they read to figure out the meanings of these words and other words that could have been used instead. For example, say, "What do you think David's mom meant when she told David to settle down?" Students will respond, "She wanted him to stop jumping on the bed and going crazy." Say, "So do you think settle down might mean to quiet down? Or calm down? Could David's mom have used those words, too?" Repeat this process for *enough* and *instant,* as well as any other words you think students need to learn in order to understand the story.

ost-reading Activity: Ask students to identify the difference between what Mom says throughout the book and what she says at the end. (She says "no" and "yes.") Ask students what it means when someone says no and what it means when someone says yes. Tell students that the words *no* and *yes* are opposites. Give examples of other opposites such as *tall/short, happy/sad,* etc. Divide students into teams and tell them they will compete against each other to figure out the opposites of words you call out. Call out a word with a clear opposite such as *night.* Give a point to the first team to say the correct answer (day). Use copies of the Opposites reproducible (page 113) for assessment or further practice.

Opposites

vocabulary reproducible for
No, David!

Name_____ Date _____

Read each word. Draw its opposite in the box beside the word.

under	
happy	
boy	

Fluency Activities
for *No, David!*

Pre-reading Activity: Tell students that David's mom is often angry because David does things he is not supposed to do. Ask students to share how their parents sound when they reprimand them for doing something wrong. Have students imitate their parents being angry. Next, ask students, "So, do you think when I read the story aloud I will sound like this?" Then, read the first page in a flat, monotone voice. Ask students to predict how you will sound when you read the book. Tell students that part of being a good reader is to use expression and voice inflections (or change how your voice sounds) to show the characters' feelings. Tell students to listen closely to determine if you sound like an angry parent as you read the story. Have students note how your voice changes when you read the last page and why.

During-reading Activity: Select volunteers to role-play the parts of Mom, David, and narrator. Do this activity in small groups. Provide each group with a copy of the book. Have the narrators begin the story with "David's mom always said . . . ." Have some students read the mom's part while the other students playing David act out the behaviors. This is an excellent activity because students love to play the silly David part as well as the stern mom. Rotate roles so that every student has an opportunity to be the mom.

Post-reading Activity: Have students reread the story while you provide clues to aid fluency as well as assess students' progress. Because the text is simple and many of the words appear more than once, even less-accomplished readers are able to read the story fluently with some prompting. Additionally, because there is no predictable pattern or rhyme, students who read focus more on the words rather than simply reciting from memory. Have students read the story chorally as you point to the words. Provide clues such as the first phoneme of the first word on each page. For example, say, "/s/." Students should reply, "Settle down!" Students may add the word *David* to most pages even when the word is not there. If this occurs, guide students to self-correct. For example, say, "Let's look at the word *David* on the cover. Do you see a word that looks like that on this page? So is Mom using David's name on this page?" This activity can be done in small groups or one-on-one. For more practice, use the No, David! reproducible (page 115) to help students practice with another set of simple text. Let students take turns reading the text and sharing their pictures.

Name_____ Date_____

Read the sentences aloud. Draw what you think David is doing in each box. Read the words and share your pictures.

No, David!	I said no!
Don't touch that, David!	**Stop that right now!**

Comprehension Activities
for *No, David!*

re-reading Activity: Prepare a piece of chart paper with three columns. Label them *Us, Predictions,* and *David.* Have students share some things they have done that have gotten them in trouble. Write these in the first column. Then, have students predict what David does to get in trouble and list those ideas in the second column. After reading the story, fill in the third column by listing the things David did to get in trouble. Compare and discuss the three columns to determine if students did any of the same things as David and if any of the predictions were right.

During-reading Activity: Provide students with an opportunity to actively read by naming story elements. Give each student a copy of the Story Elements reproducible (page 117). As you read, pause at appropriate pages and ask students to identify and list the characters, problem, and solution in the book. Discuss with students how problems are not always stated in books. Explain to students that they will state it in their own words. Let each student fill in a copy of the reproducible using dictation, illustrations, and invented spelling.

Post-reading Activity: Go back through the story and list David's behaviors that get him in trouble. As each behavior is listed, have students suggest an alternate behavior (a "good" behavior) to write down, as well. Compare the two lists and discuss issues such as consequences, rewards, following rules, self-control, etc. Ask students what they can learn from this book. Guide the discussion by asking them to notice how the book ends, how Mom feels about David, etc. Tell students that many books have messages that readers can learn from and use in their own lives. Discuss how students can use the lessons in *No, David!* in their own lives. Have students plan a sequel to *No, David!* entitled *Yes, David!* Tell students that in this book, David has learned his lesson, and now uses "good" behaviors, such as those listed earlier. Write the text cooperatively one behavior per page. Then, distribute the pages and allow each student to illustrate a page for the book. If students are able to write well enough, allow them to make individual books in which each student copies the text "Yes, David" on each page and illustrates David behaving appropriately.

Story Elements

comprehension reproducible for
No, David!

Name_____ Date _____

Follow the directions below to show what you know about the book
No, David!

Draw the characters.

Draw the problem.

Draw the solution to the problem.

SILLY SALLY
by Audrey Wood

(Harcourt Children's Books, 1992)

In this predictable rhyming book, Silly Sally walks to town "backwards" and "upside down," and encounters many silly animals that join her. Easy text and a silly story make this a favorite.

Related books: *I'm as Quick as a Cricket* by Audrey Wood (Child's Play International, Ltd., 1990); *The Napping House* by Audrey Wood (Harcourt Brace & Company, 1984); *Giggle, Giggle, Quack* by Doreen Cronin (Simon & Schuster Children's Publishing, 2002); *Duck on a Bike* by David Shannon (Blue Sky Press, 2002)

Phonemic Awareness Activities
for *Silly Sally*

Pre-reading Activity: Have students identify the initial /s/ phonemes in the title. Play charades to practice the /s/ phoneme. Explain how to play charades, then act out something that begins with /s/, such as sing, surf, etc. Let students guess what you are doing. After modeling a few times, have students take turns acting out /s/ words and let their classmates guess. (Provide the actors with /s/ words if necessary.) Further challenge students by letting two teams have a competition. Let students act out words that start with the /s/ phoneme and others that do not. Have students determine which words are /s/ words. For another variation, after students can hear the /s/ phonemes at the beginnings of words, act out words that have /s/ phonemes in the middle or end. After students guess, discuss where in the words the /s/ sound can be heard. You can also vary the activity by letting students play charades in small groups or pairs.

During-reading Activity: Ask students to identify the beginning sound in Sally's name. Point out to students what their mouths "look" and "feel" like when they make the /s/ sound. As you reread the story, tell students to listen for words that begin with the same beginning sound as *Sally*. Instruct students to identify /s/ words by making the /s/ sound like a snake. Use copies of the S-s-s Sound reproducible (page 119) to provide further practice or assess students' awareness of the sound.

Post-reading Activity: Find the rhyming words on each page of *Silly Sally*. Demonstrate how to change a word by changing its initial phoneme. Say, "What happens to the word *pig* when the author changes the /p/ to /j/? P-p-pig, j-j-jig." (If students have difficulty identifying that *pig* changes to *jig*, review before continuing.) Then say, "Now let's try it with /b/. B-b-ig, b-b-ig." Have students repeat the sounds, then ask, "What word does that make?" Depending on your students' understanding of this concept, continue to manipulate initial phonemes with these words or try other rhyming word pairs in the book (*dog/frog, loon/tune*, etc.). Because the focus is on identifying and changing initial phonemes, creating nonsense words is acceptable.

S-s-s Sound

phonemic awareness reproducible for
Silly Sally

Name_____ Date _____

In each row, draw an x on the picture that has a name that does not start with the /s/ sound.

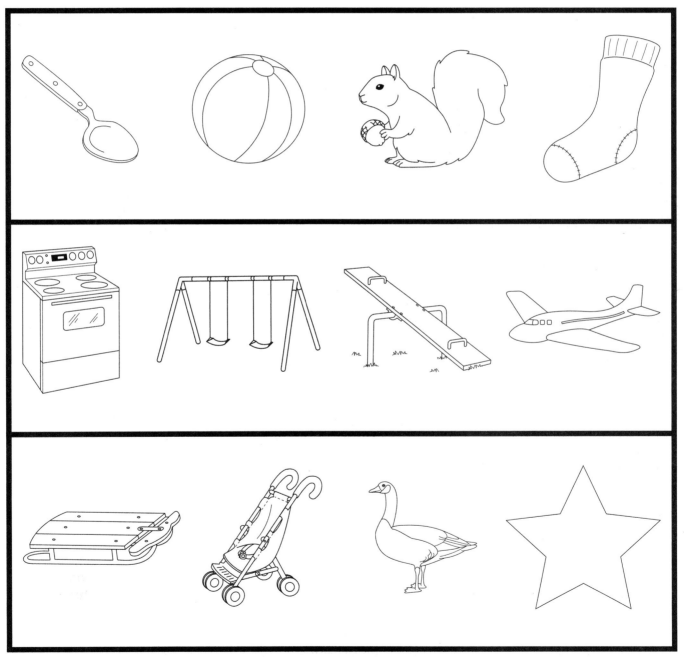

Phonics Activities
for *Silly Sally*

Pre-reading Activity: Direct students to make words with onsets and rimes by using words from the book as a basis (*pig/jig, dog/frog, sheep/sleep,* and *town/down*). On index cards, write onsets and rimes from the book (d, j, p, t, fr, sh, sl; eep, ig, og, own). (You may want to skip *loon* and *tune* due to their different spellings.) Tell students that they will read words using the same endings (or families) but different beginnings. Explain that they will see these words later in the story. Place the rimes in a pocket chart or display them on the board with tape or magnets. Read a rime, then add each different onset and read the new words. Have students repeat each onset, then the rimes and the words after you say them. To extend the activity, let students read and write new words by creating more word cards with different onsets and adding them to the same rimes. Some possible onset/rime combinations are l-og, h-og, sw-eep, and cr-eep. Use copies of the Onsets reproducible (page 121) for assessment or further practice.

During-reading Activity: This messy activity is fun for students and gives them a concrete reference for the /s/ sound. Boil a package of spaghetti and add a small amount of vegetable oil to the water. Drain and cool the spaghetti and store it in a resealable, plastic bag overnight. Tell students that they will be spelling with "*Silly Sally* spaghetti." Distribute the spaghetti to students, along with sheets of waxed paper. Have students say the word *spaghetti* with an emphasis on the /s/. As you read, pause each time you say the /s/ sound. Have each student use two strands of spaghetti to make an /s/ each time she hears the blend. At the end of the book, count students' spaghetti to see how many times they heard the /s/ sound. If time permits, have them use the spaghetti to create other initial letters as they listen to the book.

Post-reading Activity: Ask any students whose names begin with the same letter as Sally to come to the front of the classroom. Say their names adding the word silly ("Silly Steven"). Tell students that they will write their own versions of *Silly Sally* using their names, but that first they must figure out a way for everyone's name to start with the letter s. Ask students how their names would sound if they all started with the letter s. Use your own name or another student's name as an example to help guide them through this thought process. Help each student "change" his name for the day. Although this may take a little time, students really enjoy the silliness of this activity! For students whose names begin with vowels, guide students to discover that their names are easier to pronounce if they add the s to the beginnings (such as Eric/Seric or Audrey/Saudrey). For names with consonants, either create a blend with the s (Torie/Storie) or drop the initial letter and add s (Richard/Sichard). Write each student's name on a piece of chart paper with the "new" spelling as you go around the room. Then, have each student create her own version of *Silly Sally* by copying the sentence with her "new" name. For example, Liz would write *Silly Siz went to town, walking backwards, upside down.* She should then draw herself walking backwards and upside down. Display the work on a bulletin board or compile as a class book titled *Silly Students.*

Onsets

phonics reproducible for
Silly Sally

Name_____ Date _____

Circle the correct beginning letter for each picture. Then, complete the words by writing the letters on the lines.

p j __ig	h d __og
c b __at	j r __et
s c __up	f s __un

Vocabulary Activities
for *Silly Sally*

Pre-reading Activity: Give students an opportunity to identify nouns and also expose them to words they will encounter in the book. Explain to students that a *noun* is a person, place, or thing and that on each page of the story they will "meet" a new noun. On the board, copy a phrase from the book such as *On the way she met a pig.* Have individual students underline or circle each person, place, or thing in the sentence. Nouns are a fairly advanced concept for this age, so evaluate students' abilities before introducing them to pronouns, like *she.*

During-reading Activity: Introduce or review the concept of verbs by explaining to students that a *verb* is a word that shows action. Ask for volunteers to demonstrate some examples of actions. As you read the story, pause and have students identify action words such as *went, walking, met,* etc. When students find a verb, list it on the board and have students act it out. As an extension, use the Act It Out reproducible (page 123) to continue teaching students the concept of verbs. Cut apart the cards and distribute them randomly to students. Choose one student to act out her card. Explain that she must act out only the word on the card. On the board, write the verbs students guess correctly in one column and correctly guessed nouns in another column. Do not label the columns. After each student has acted out a word, discuss the differences between the words in the two columns.

Post-reading Activity: Ask students to tell what Sally is like. When students say, "silly," ask them to explain what would make a person silly. Then, ask students to describe themselves. Guide them to use descriptive words. For example, if a student says that he likes to run fast, respond, "So one word that you would use to describe yourself might be *fast.*" Make a web of descriptive words on a piece of chart paper. Explain to students that these words describe them, and they are called *adjectives.* Have each student write the adjective that best describes him with his name (*Fast Ben*) and illustrate himself appropriately. As a variation, introduce the concept of alliteration and have students think of adjectives that begin with the same letters as their names (Energetic Erica, Smart Simon, etc.).

First-Rate Reading™ Grade K • CD-0068 • © Carson-Dellosa

Act It Out

vocabulary reproducible for
Silly Sally

Name_____ Date _____

Cut out the cards. Distribute them to students for use with the vocabulary during-reading activity (page 122).

skip	run	jump
eat	laugh	wash
dance	wiggle	dog
snake	car	bee
doctor	teacher	student

Fluency Activities
for *Silly Sally*

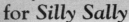re-reading Activity: Use the passage on the I've Got Rhythm reproducible (page 125) to practice fluency and get students used to the rhythm of the story's text. Cut copies of the reproducible in half and distribute one to each student. Read the passage aloud, have students read it chorally, then direct each student to work with a partner to practice reading the passage fluently. This will be a helpful activity for students because the text is very simple and will help students recognize words later on in the story.

During-reading Activity: Divide students into homogenous groups and assign roles (Sally, pig, dog, frog, loon, sheep, Neddy Buttercup, and narrator). Have students practice reading and performing the story. Have groups take turns performing the book for another class or for visitors. As students become more familiar with the book, consider rotating roles so that each student has an opportunity to read the part of the narrator.

Post-reading Activity: Students benefit greatly from having individual attention paid to their fluency. *Silly Sally's* simple language and easy rhythm make this book excellent for fluency practice. Read one-on-one with each student while focusing on fluency. Create a special read-with-an-adult center that students look forward to visiting. Place copies of *Silly Sally* at the center and choose different students to visit the center while other students work independently on an activity. Either read with the students or have an adult volunteer come in to read. Different reading strategies include:
* choral reading—adult and student read story in unison
* echo reading—adult reads a line, then student echoes the line
* my side/your side reading—the adult reads the pages on "her side" while student reads pages on "his side"
* student reads while adult offers praise and feedback

Name_____   Date _____

Silly Sally went to town.

On the way, she met a silly pig,

a silly dog,

a silly loon,

and a silly sheep.

Silly Sally went to town.

- -

Name_____   Date _____

Silly Sally went to town.

On the way, she met a silly pig,

a silly dog,

a silly loon,

and a silly sheep.

Silly Sally went to town.

Comprehension Activities
for *Silly Sally*

Pre-reading Activity: Ask students to form predictions based on the book title and cover. Ask students what they think Sally will do that will make her so silly, where she is going, etc. Have students use copies of the *Silly Sally* Predictions reproducible (page 127) to write or draw their individual predictions. Then, have students share their answers. After reading, revisit the predictions and confirm predictions that came true. Have students indicate whether their predictions were right, kind of right, or wrong, then draw pictures to show what the story was really about. Explain how predicting can help a reader understand a story better by setting a purpose (or "getting your brain ready") before reading. Stress that the importance of predicting is not whether a prediction is correct, but whether it helps them understand the story and be active readers.

During-reading Activity: While reading, pause at appropriate pages and reinforce active reading skills by asking students, "Who is the main character in the story? Where is Sally going? Who do you think Sally will meet next? (Have students look for picture clues.) What kind of person do you think Sally is? Why do you think Sally walks backwards and upside down?" For the last question, ask students if they can think of occasions that would make them walk upside down.

Post-reading Activity: If students think Sally's way of walking to town is strange, ask them, "What must the people in the town think? What would have happened if Neddy Buttercup never came along?" Have students write "sequels" to the book by imagining what happened once Sally arrived in town with her animal friends and Neddy walking upside down. Ask students, "Would everyone join her? Would she get in trouble?" Let students either dictate or draw sequels to the story. Post them on a bulletin board titled *Whatever Happened to Silly Sally?*

First-Rate Reading™ Grade K • CD-0068 • © Carson-Dellosa

Silly Sally **Predictions**

comprehension reproducible for
Silly Sally

Name_____ Date _____

I predict that the book *Silly Sally* will be about_____

_____

Draw what you think will happen in the box below.

Circle one: My prediction was   right.   kind of right.   wrong.
Draw what really happened in the story in the box below.

There Was an Old Lady Who Swallowed a Fly

by Simms Taback

(Viking, 1997)

The well-known story of an old lady who accidentally swallowed a fly is retold in this cumulative storybook. The lady then proceeds to swallow other animals, such as a bird and cat, in an attempt to catch the animals she previously swallowed. The predictable rhythm and rhyme naturally inspire children to read or sing along.

Related books: *I Know an Old Lady Who Swallowed a Fly* by Nadine B. Westcott (Little, Brown & Company, 1980); *This Is the House That Jack Built* by Pam Adams (Child's Play International, Ltd., 1989); *I Know an Old Lady Who Swallowed a Pie* by Alison Jackson (Dutton Books, 1997)

Phonemic Awareness Activities
for *There Was an Old Lady Who Swallowed a Fly*

Pre-reading Activity: Introduce or review the long /i/ sound. Say the words *I*, *why*, *fly*, and *die* from the story, pausing to stress the long /i/ sound in each. Have students repeat the words. Tell students to notice how their mouths, lips, and tongues "feel" and "look" while forming this phoneme. Say other words that have the long /i/ sound (*kite*, *pie*, *bye*, etc.), stressing the /i/ phoneme each time. Tell students to listen as you talk, and identify when they hear the long /i/ phoneme by saluting like a sailor and saying, "Aye-aye!" Encourage students to look for long /i/ words in the book.

During-reading Activity: Work on different rhymes on each page. Read the story and pause after each page. Have students identify the rhyming words by repeating them and thinking of at least one new rhyming word for each. For example, say, "Imagine that! She swallowed a cat." Students should respond with, "That, cat." Ask, "Can you think of a new rhyming word for that pair?" Students may respond with, "Hat!"

Post-reading Activity: Use the Name That Phoneme reproducible (page 129) to give students an opportunity to identify phonemes in words from the story. Copy and distribute the reproducible. Have students work in pairs or small groups to identify the phonemes for each picture. Have students identify the initial phonemes or the ending phonemes, or divide the words into individual phonemes. Have them sound-spell each word and write the words on the lines.

Name That Phoneme

phonemic awareness reproducible for
There Was an Old Lady Who Swallowed a Fly

Name_____ Date _____

With a partner or your group, say each word slowly. Write the words' sounds on the lines.

_____ _____

_____

_____

_____

_____

_____

 _____

Phonics Activities

for *There Was an Old Lady Who Swallowed a Fly*

Pre-reading Activity: Read the book's title aloud. Explain that in the title, the letter y makes two different sounds: the long /e/ sound as in the word *lady*, and the long /i/ sound in the word *fly*. Copy and distribute the Letter Y Song reproducible (page 131) for students. Sing the song with them. Then, use the bottom half of the reproducible to assess students' understanding of the two different sounds for the letter y. Review what sounds long e and long i make before assigning the reproducible.

During-reading Activity: Teach students about the different ways to use letters to show the long /o/ sound. Write the word *swallow* on the board. Have students say the word and then swallow to show they know what it means. Ask them to help you think of other words with the long /o/ sound. On the board, write three headings for columns. Label one column *ow*, one *o_e*, and one *oa*. (If your students are not ready for the silent e, leave it out.) As students call out words that also have the long /o/ sound, list them in the appropriate columns. For example, list *blow* under the *ow* header, *bone* under the *o_e* header, and *boat* under the *oa* header. When you have several words for each column, write the words on index cards. Mix up the word cards, place them in a center, and let students take turns sorting the long /o/ words.

Post-reading Activity: Respond to the story by writing a class alphabet version of the book. Review the alphabet letters and sounds by collaborating on a class book entitled *There Was an Old Lady Who Swallowed the ABC's!* Have students complete the sentence "There was an old lady who swallowed a ____" with a word that begins with each letter of the alphabet. Repeat several times with different students volunteering answers. You may want to stay with the animal theme, try a new theme such as foods, or not follow a particular theme at all. Once an item has been listed for each letter of the alphabet, let students reread the sentences with you, plugging in the class responses for each letter. ("There was an old lady who swallowed an apple. There was an old lady who swallowed a brownie.") Assign each student a different letter and have him copy the sentence and illustrate it.

Letter Y Song
phonics reproducible for
There Was an Old Lady Who Swallowed a Fly

Name _____ Date _____

Sing this song to the tune of "Old MacDonald."

The letter y it makes two sounds:
e - i - e - i - e!
When it is used as a vowel:
e - i - e - i - e!
If you say lady, then say fly,
You'll hear both the e and i!
The letter y it makes two sounds:
e - i - e - i - e!

Look at the pictures. Write the letter y in each blank. Then, circle the sound the y makes in each word.

kitt__   long e   long i

cr__   long e   long i

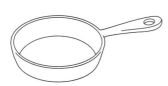

fr__ ing pan   long e   long i

bab__   long e   long i

Vocabulary Activities
for *There Was an Old Lady Who Swallowed a Fly*

Pre-reading Activity: Teach critical vocabulary prior to reading the story. After reading the title, ask students what *swallowed* means. Have them give examples and use the word in sentences. Ask students what they think of someone swallowing a fly. Ask them if they think it is absurd or crazy (or gross!). Tell them that in the book, the narrator also thinks it's absurd. Tell students to look for the words *absurd* and *swallow* as you read the book aloud.

During-reading Activity: Make word cards with the following vocabulary words: *fly, spider, bird, cat, dog, cow, horse, swallowed, die, wiggled, jiggled, tickled, catch,* and the words *the, a,* and *and.* Mix up the word cards and tell students that some are animal word cards and some are action word cards. Show each card to students as you read the word and have students repeat it. Distribute cards randomly to students and tell them to hold up their cards when you read their words. Afterwards, sort the cards according to animal or action. Cards can be sorted by having one student volunteer to collect the animal cards and another collect the action cards. Or, use magnetic tape to attach cards to the board under sentence strips labeled *Animal Words* and *Action Words.* Once the cards are sorted, store them in two labeled resealable, plastic bags or envelopes. Place the cards in a center and encourage students to mix and match them to make new sentences such as *The horse wiggled,* or *The cat swallowed the spider,* or *The bird tickled the cow.*

Post-reading Activity: After students are familiar with the story and have practiced recognizing, sorting, and reading the vocabulary words, use copies of the Animal Match reproducible (page 133) for assessment. Have students match the animal vocabulary words to the correct animal pictures. This will assess students' recognition of each word out of context. For a more hands-on version of this activity, provide a toy version of each animal. Use a marker to divide a sheet of paper into seven sections, then write each word in a section. Place the toys and sectioned paper in a center and let each student place each toy on the correct section with its matching word.

Animal Match
vocabulary reproducible for
There Was an Old Lady Who Swallowed a Fly

Name_____ Date _____

Draw a line to match each word to its picture.

fly

spider

bird

cat

dog

cow

horse

Fluency Activities

for *There Was an Old Lady Who Swallowed a Fly*

Pre-reading Activity: Demonstrate how boring it would be to listen to someone read aloud in a non-fluent manner (slow, choppy, monotone) using the first page of the book's text. Have students compare as you reread the same text in a fluent, excited, rhythmic manner. Tell students that they will practice reading fluently by joining in with the two repetitive lines, "I don't know why she swallowed a fly. Perhaps she'll die." Have students demonstrate how they will recite these lines fluently and rhythmically. Practice a few times. Give each student an opportunity to demonstrate how she can recite them fluently. Praise expressive, clear readers. Then, tell students to listen for those lines and join in fluently when they are read.

During-reading Activity: Divide the class into two groups. Have one group read the first line about each new animal: "There was an old lady who swallowed a spider." (*There Was an Old Lady Who Swallowed a Fly*, page 5), and the other group read each follow-up line: "That wiggled and jiggled and tickled inside her." (*There Was an Old Lady Who Swallowed a Fly*, page 6). Have both groups read the rest of the verses. Let the class read the book aloud without adding movement. Then, have the first group act out swallowing increasingly larger animals as they read and have the second group act out the action words. Students will find this very funny; the challenge will be to have them continue to read fluently.

Post-reading Activity: Use this creative activity to ensure that children read aloud at home. Reread the story while putting the animals in the lady's belly! Copy the Old Lady and Animals reproducible (page 135) on sturdy paper for each student, and have students color and cut out the characters. Give each student a resealable, plastic bag. Show students how to cut out the old lady's belly. Consider laminating the old lady and cutting out the laminate from the "belly" so that this pattern will be more durable. Attach a plastic sandwich bag to the back of the character with tape or staples. (A bag that has a foldover top will work better than a resealable bag.) Make sure that the opening of each bag covers the opening in the old lady's belly so that when a student puts the other characters "into" the old lady's belly, they will fall into the plastic bag. Have each student practice reading the story and placing each animal into the old lady's belly as it is read. (They will need to roll or fold the horse and cow patterns slightly to get them to fit.) Remind students to read with expression and fluidity. Then, encourage students to take the puppets home and read for family members. Ask each student to let his family put the animals into the old lady's belly so he can focus on the reading. Family members will probably want to sing the familiar tune, so tell students that singing the song is also fine.

Old Lady and Animals
fluency reproducible for
There Was an Old Lady Who Swallowed a Fly

Name_____ Date _____

Color and cut out each picture. Cut out the hole in the old lady and attach a plastic bag to make a belly. Place the animals in the bag as you read the book.

Comprehension Activities
for *There Was An Old Lady Who Swallowed a Fly*

Pre-reading Activity: Set a purpose for reading with this activity. Read the title to the class. Ask students if they know anyone who eats flies. Brainstorm a list of things students eat and another list of things they wouldn't eat. Tell students that you will read the story aloud to find out if the old lady eats things from either list. Revisit the lists after reading and circle items that were found in the story.

During-reading Activity: While you are reading, draw and fill in a time line on a piece of chart paper or the board to identify the sequence of events in the story. After reading the first page, ask students what you should write first. Then, pause after each subsequent page to discuss and add the next event to the diagram. After completing the diagram, discuss what a food chain is, and ask students if they think this food chain can really happen. Discuss why or why not.

Post-reading Activity: Ask students to share their opinions about the book. Explain that it is acceptable for them to dislike or like a reading selection, but they need to think about why. Ask students why they liked or disliked *There Was an Old Lady Who Swallowed a Fly*. Allow each student to use the Journal Entry reproducible (page 137) to respond to the story. Let students use illustrations, invented spelling, dictation, word walls, premade charts, etc. Or, allow students to form groups with other students who share their opinion and to make lists of reasons for their choices. Have students share their entries with partners or with the class.

Journal Entry

comprehension reproducible for
There Was an Old Lady Who Swallowed a Fly

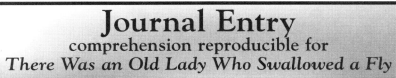

Name_____ Date _____

Circle the word and picture that tells whether you like or dislike the book. Write reasons for your answer on the lines, then draw a picture about your answer.

I   like   dislike   the story because _____

_____

_____

_____

The Very Hungry Caterpillar
by Eric Carle

(Philomel Books, 1969)

This easy-to-follow story describes the life of a caterpillar as it emerges from its egg and proceeds to eat a variety of foods during the course of a week. After making its cocoon, it emerges as a beautiful butterfly. Use this book to teach number words, days of the week, sequence of events, and of course, a butterfly's life cycle.

Related books: *The Very Lonely Firefly* by Eric Carle (Philomel Books, 1999); *The Very Busy Spider* by Eric Carle (Philomel Books, 1995); *The Very Quiet Cricket* by Eric Carle (Philomel Books, 1990)

Phonemic Awareness Activities
for *The Very Hungry Caterpillar*

Pre-reading Activity: Review initial consonant phonemes. Conceal the book's cover and read the title for students to repeat. Ask what phonemes they hear at the beginning of each word (/th/, /v/, /h/, /k/). Ask students what letters they will see on the cover that will make those sounds (if students have not learned the consonant digraph th, skip *the*). Show the title to students to confirm their responses. Have each student name three other words that begin with each phoneme.

During-reading Activity: Give a real-life example of an exception, such as "Students may not eat in class, except when there is a party." Explain that letters don't always make their usual sounds, and these are called *exceptions*. Ask students to give examples of the two sounds the vowel o usually makes. Tell students that the words *moon*, *on*, *one*, *of*, *look*, *to*, *food*, *oranges*, *cone*, *cocoon*, and *hole* are all in *The Very Hungry Caterpillar* and all contain the letter o. Write the word *one* on the board. Read it aloud and ask what letter the word starts with. Then, ask if the letter o makes its usual sound in *one* and what sound they hear at the beginning of the word *one* (w). Explain that this is an exception, and there are other exceptions, too. Demonstrate the same exercise with *to* and *look*. If you have discussed sight words or high-frequency words, mention that exceptions are one reason it is important to read some words "on sight" instead of sounding them out. As you read the book, pause at words containing the letter o. Have students point out the different /o/ phonemes.

Post-reading Activity: Review that the caterpillar was hungry at the beginning of the story and turned into a butterfly at the end. Write *hungry* and *butterfly* on the board. Ask what letter is at the end of both words. Ask students what phoneme the y makes in *hungry* (long /e/) and in *butterfly* (long /i/). Explain that y can act like both a consonant and a vowel. Review what phoneme the letter y makes as a consonant (as in *yellow*). Read the Sounds That Y Makes reproducible (page 139) aloud, then help students sort the y words according to one of the three phonemes: /y/ as in *yellow*, long /i/ as in *butterfly*, or long /e/ as in hungry.

Sounds That Y Makes

phonemic awareness reproducible for
The Very Hungry Caterpillar

Name _____   Date _____

Sometimes the letter y makes the y sound like the color yellow. Color the sun yellow.

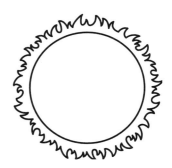

Sometimes the letter y makes the long e sound like the words very hungry. Color the very hungry caterpillar green.

Sometimes the letter y makes the long i sound like the word butterfly. Color the butterfly red.

Listen as your teacher reads the words. If the y makes the y sound like in the word yellow, circle it in yellow. If the y makes the long e sound like in the word green, circle it in green. If the y makes the long i sound like in the word butterfly, circle it in red.

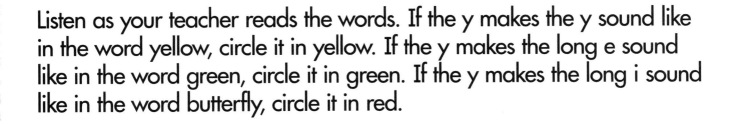

tiny	cry	yo-yo	happy	grouchy	why
yes	busy	my	yell	shy	yard

Phonics Activities
for *The Very Hungry Caterpillar*

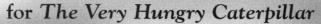

Pre-reading Activity: In this activity, students practice phonics skills, use phonics knowledge to record ideas in writing, and predict what they will read in the book. Explain that this book is about a hungry caterpillar who eats different foods on different days of the week. Tell students that they will predict what foods the caterpillar eats according to phonics clues you give them. Give each student a copy of the Caterpillar Foods reproducible (page 141). Tell students to use the clues you give them to write their guesses for each day. Say, "On Monday, the caterpillar eats something that starts with the short /a/ sound. Write or draw all of the foods you can think of that begin with the short /a/ sound in the first box titled Monday." (If students are not writing yet, have them brainstorm answers as you write them on the board. Be sure to say the short /a/ sound for them and have them repeat it.) After a few minutes, let students share their prediction lists for Monday. Continue with each day by giving the first phoneme as the clue for each food. For words that begin with blends (*plums, strawberries*) or digraphs (*cheese, chocolate, cherry*), be sure to give the blend or digraph phoneme as the clue—not the names of the letters ("On Wednesday, the caterpillar eats something that begins with /pl/. What foods can you think of that begin with the blend /pl/?")

During-reading Activity: To prepare for this big book activity, cover the rimes of some words in the text with sticky notes. (If you do not have a big book version, write on the board the sentences containing words you want students to work with.) The words you choose to cover will depend on your students' levels, previous lessons, and the objectives you wish to accomplish. For example, if you want students to practice using initial phoneme clues to identify and read words, select words such as *food* and *day*. If you want to emphasize blends, cover rimes in words such as *plums, strawberries*, etc. Then, write each covered word on an index card. Tell students that parts of some words in the text are covered, and it will be their job to figure out which words belong there. Randomly distribute the word cards. Tell students that as you read and come to a partially covered word, they should read their word cards to see if the words they are holding could be the covered word. If it is, have the student stand up and hold up his card. Sound out the student's word and point out the phonics characteristic you chose to emphasize. Then, reread the sentence and replace the partially covered word with the word on the student's card. Have students determine if that word is, in fact, the missing word. Confirm by removing the sticky note and matching the word in the text to the word card.

Post-reading Activity: Use days of the week for phonics instruction. Give each student six sheets of paper for the inside pages of a book and two sheets of construction paper for covers. Have each student title her book *The Very Hungry Student*, and add a self-portrait and her name to the front cover. On the board, write the sentence *On Monday I ate m_____*. Have students copy the sentence and draw or write about things they ate on Monday that start with m such as mangoes, marshmallows, etc. Repeat with t for Tuesday, w for Wednesday, th for Thursday (allow silly items here, since there are few th food words, such as thousand-island dressing, Thanksgiving food, three-bean salad, etc.), f for Friday, and s for Saturday and Sunday (use one page for these days since they start with the same letter). Have students staple their pages and covers together to create books. The following Monday, let students share their m pages. Provide a few m-foods for a taste test (get parental permission first). Repeat for the other days.

Caterpillar Foods

phonics reproducible for
The Very Hungry Caterpillar

Name_____ Date _____

Listen to your teacher read clues about what the caterpillar eats each day. Write or draw your guesses in the boxes.

Monday	Tuesday

Wednesday	Thursday

Friday	Saturday

Vocabulary Activities
for *The Very Hungry Caterpillar*

Pre-reading Activity: Prior to reading the story, teach students the life cycle of a butterfly and corresponding vocabulary words such as *egg, caterpillar,* and *cocoon.* Have students use these vocabulary words to illustrate butterfly life cycles and establish prior knowledge for the story. Give each student four index cards. Draw the cycle on a piece of chart paper for students to refer to or create one when explaining the vocabulary words. On the first card have each student write *#1 egg,* then draw an egg on a leaf. On the second card, have students write *#2 caterpillar,* then draw a caterpillar. Repeat for cards *#3* (*cocoon*) and *#4* (*butterfly*). Have students review the stages of the life cycle and use vocabulary terms by flipping through the cards. Students can also use the cards during reading to refer to each stage as the very hungry caterpillar changes into a cocoon and then a butterfly.

During-reading Activity: As you read the story, pause on the word *Sunday.* Ask students what they notice about the way this word is written in the sentence. (It begins with an uppercase letter.) Explain that names of people, places, or things are called proper nouns. Tell students that names of the days of the week always begin with uppercase letters, just like students' names. Have students identify the other names of the days of the week as you read, and identify the letters that are uppercase and why. Extend the activity by having students list other names of specific people, places, and things and list them on the board using uppercase letters.

Post-reading Activity: Because number words are often found in text, it is important for students to recognize these words. Review the foods the caterpillar ate in the story and emphasize how many of each item were eaten. The Number Words Games reproducible (page 143) provides students with practice in identifying and reading the number words in the story. It can be used for two games. For the first game, pair students and give each pair a copy of the reproducible. Review the number and kinds of objects the caterpillar ate (through the number five). Have students draw the correct number of objects in each box, color the objects, then cut out the cards. Have them play memory (concentration) by placing the cards facedown, and taking turns flipping over two at a time to find matches between the number words and the number of objects in the pictures. For the second game, draw the correct number of objects. Make enough copies so that you can give each student one word or picture card. Cut out the cards and distribute them randomly to students. Have students cover their cards until you say, "Go." When you say "go," instruct students to look at their cards, then hold them up so that other students can see. Students should then try to find other students with matching cards. For example, a student with a picture card showing one apple must find a partner holding the word cards for *one.* Time the game and either award points to students who found their partners in the allotted time, give enough time for everyone to find his partner, or award the first five pairs. Repeat the game by collecting and shuffling the cards, then redistributing them.

Number Words Games
vocabulary reproducible for
The Very Hungry Caterpillar

Name_____ Date _____

In each box, draw the objects and number of objects the caterpillar ate. Cut apart the cards.

one

two

three

four

five

Fluency Activities
for *The Very Hungry Caterpillar*

Pre-reading Activity: Expose students to the story format and give them an opportunity to practice fluency by using the I Ate Many Apples reproducible (page 145). Because the poem's text is simple and repetitive, students will learn it quickly. Make a transparency or poster-size copy, and give each student his own copy. While tracking print, read the poem for students. Reread it, this time encouraging students to use their fingers to point to each word (track print). Reread it a third time, with students echo reading the poem. Next, have students read it chorally with you. Then, have students read the day-of-the-week half of each line, while you respond with the second half of each line. Finally, pair students and have them practice reading it aloud to each other.

During-reading Activity: Prior to this activity, copy a few sentences from the story on sentence strips, then cut each word apart. As you read the story, pause on the page that contains one of the copied sentences and select students to hold the word cards in scrambled order. Have the class read the words in scrambled order and ask them if that "sounds right" and makes sense. Instruct the cardholders to change their order. Reread the "sentence" as is. Ask students again if it "sounds right" and makes sense. Direct students to unscramble themselves so that their sentence makes sense and sounds right. Encourage the class to help them. When the words are in the correct order, have students read the words aloud in a fluent manner. Repeat for the other sentences you selected. Then, reread the book and let students chorally read the selected sentences with you.

Post-reading Activity: Some students will be able to learn to read parts of this book themselves. To help them, show them how to track print. Provide a big book version of *The Very Hungry Caterpillar* or work with individual students. Demonstrate how to use your index finger to track text. Explain that their fingers move across the pages to help them follow the words just like a hungry caterpillar follows food. Practice making caterpillar movements with fingers, then let each student use his index finger to track some text and read it aloud.

I Ate Many Apples

fluency reproducible for
The Very Hungry Caterpillar

Name_____ Date _____

Use this poem about apples to practice reading aloud.

I Ate Many Apples

On Monday, I ate one apple. It tasted very good.

On Tuesday, I ate two apples, because I knew I could!

On Wednesday, I ate three apples: one yellow, one green, one red.

On Thursday, I ate four apples, and then I went to bed.

On Friday, I ate five apples. They were tart and sweet.

On Saturday, I ate six apples. That was all I could eat.

On Sunday I ate seven apples, and got a stomachache!

Today I will eat no apples, and give myself a break.

Comprehension Activities
for *The Very Hungry Caterpillar*

Pre-reading Activity: Help students set a purpose for reading and make predictions. Prior to reading the story, take a "book walk" with the class. Show students each page and encourage them to share what they see and think is happening in the story. Ask students to use illustrations to predict what words they might encounter in the text. As students offer suggestions, list them on the board. Revisit the list as or after you read. Put a check mark next to each word that appears in the text, and an x next to each word that does not.

During-reading Activity: Give each student a copy of the Personal Puppet Show reproducible (page 147), and tell students that as you read the book, they will conduct "puppet shows" at their desks. Let students color and cut out the patterns. Have students monitor their reading comprehension and actively listen to the story by "acting" out the story with patterns. For example, as you begin to read, have each student pick up the egg cutout and place it on the leaf cutout and place the moon cutout toward the top of her desk. As you continue to read, each student should replace the egg, leaf, and moon cutout with the caterpillar and sun cutouts. Pause appropriately in order to give students an opportunity to keep up and "act out" the scenes at their desks. Encourage students to add sound effects, as you read, such as the caterpillar munching on the apple and groaning when he has a stomachache.

Post-reading Activity: Show students the illustrations and tell them that the author used a collage technique by cutting out shapes and drawings from colored paper and pasting them on white paper. Tell students that they will retell the story using Eric Carle's collage technique. Give students construction paper, tissue paper, and other supplies. Reread the story and let each student choose a food object from the story to illustrate. Help students tear the paper and assemble their objects by gluing them on white paper. Read the story again and let students hold up their paper creations as they hear the names of their objects read aloud. Post the pictures on a bulletin board titled *Caterpillar Food*.

Personal Puppet Show

comprehension reproducible for
The Very Hungry Caterpillar

Name _____ Date _____

Color and cut apart the cards. Use them to act out the story as your teacher reads.

Where the Wild Things Are
by Maurice Sendak

(HarperCollins Publishers, 1963)

Students love the classic story of Max, a little boy who gets sent to bed without supper for acting like a "wild thing." In his room, he grows a forest, sails across an ocean, and becomes king of the "wild things." But, Max misses home and returns to find his supper waiting for him.

Related books: *Blueberries for Sal* by Robert McCloskey (Puffin, 1976); *Harold and the Purple Crayon* by Crockett Johnson (HarperCollins, 1955); *In the Night Kitchen* by Maurice Sendak (HarperCollins, 1996)

Phonemic Awareness Activities
for *Where the Wild Things Are*

Pre-reading Activity: Practice identifying the /w/ sound while introducing story words. Read the book title aloud and have students repeat it. Ask what sound the word *wild* begins with. Then, read the word *the*, and ask if *wild* and *the* begin with the same sound. Repeat for each word in the title. (You may also use *where* if your phonics program and regional dialect consider this the /w/ and not /wh/ sound. After students have identified the two words in the title that begin with the /w/, say other words found in the book such as *night, wore, wolf, mischief, without, forest, walls, world, ocean*, etc. Have students identify if they begin with the same sound as *where* and *wild*.

During-reading Activity: Pause when the name *Max* first appears in the text. Have students repeat it. Ask them what letter makes the /ks/ sound at the end (x). Have students repeat the following words after you: *fox, box, rocks, blocks*. Ask students what phoneme all of those words have in common (the /ks/ sound at the end). Demonstrate how to hold two index fingers over each other to make an "x." Each time a student hears Max's name, have her indicate that she has heard the /ks/ sound by making an "x" with her fingers.

Post-reading Activity: Ask students what Max's mother calls him (wild thing). Write *wild thing* on the board and ask what letter is the same in both words (letter i). After students answer, ask what is different about the sounds the letter i makes. Explain that the letter i makes the long /i/ sound in *wild* and the long /e/ or short /i/ sound in *thing*. (Some phonics programs teach that ing and ink endings contain short /i/ phonemes. If your program teaches that this is the long /e/ sound, focus on a different short /i/ story word, such as *mischief*.) Play the "Wild Thing Game." Have students line up in two teams. Enlarge the I-Words reproducible (page 149). Cut apart the cards. Cover the word with your finger and show a card to a player from the first team. Have him say the picture name, uncover the word, and decide if it has a short or long /i/ sound. If he is correct, give that team the card. Give the other team a turn. The team with the most cards wins. Dance like "wild things" when the game is finished.

Name_____ Date _____

Cut apart the cards. Use them with the phonemic awareness post-reading activity (page 148).

ice	kite	bike	lion
tiger	fish	picture	mitt
zipper	kitten	lightbulb	pie
valentine	bib	crib	pickle

Phonics Activities
for *Where the Wild Things Are*

Pre-reading Activity: This activity correlates with the pre-reading phonemic awareness activity (page 148). Note that how you expect students to pronounce these words may be affected by your phonics program and local dialect preferences. Point out the w words in the title (*where and wild*). After students have identified /w/ words, have them brainstorm a class list of words that begin with the letter w. Let each student illustrate one w word of his choice. Use yarn to create a giant web on a bulletin board. Make sure students understand that the word *web* begins with the letter w. Place students' illustrations on the bulletin board.

During-reading Activity: Point out to students that the title contains two words that begin with consonant digraphs (*where* and *things*). Explain that a consonant digraph is when two consonants are put together to make a new sound, then review sounds t and h make when separate, as well as the w and h. Then, compare these to the sounds at the beginning of the words *where* and *thing*. Tell students that these two digraphs are very popular and they like to join in on all of the "wild parties" that the "wild things" have, so the two digraphs will appear in the book often. Divide a piece of chart paper in half vertically, label one column *wh* and the other *th*. Tell students to look or listen for the two digraphs as you read the story. When you read a word that contains one of them, such as *the, another, without, anything, where,* etc., have students raise their hands to indicate they have seen or heard a digraph. Then, write the word in the correct column and underline the digraph. Have students repeat the word, identify the digraph, and say the sound the digraph makes.

Post-reading Activity: Tell students that Max used his imagination to become king of the wild things. Write the words *thing* and *king* on the board. Ask students what these two words have in common (ing ending). Explain that these words are part of the ing word family. Distribute copies of the King of Things reproducible (page 151) to students. Have students fill in the missing letters which match the pictures by labeling objects in the ing family. You may wish to direct this activity to the whole class or to groups, depending on students' skills and reading levels.

King of Things

phonics reproducible for
Where the Wild Things Are

Name_____ Date _____

Look at each picture. Write the letter or letters in the blanks to make words that name each picture. Color the pictures.

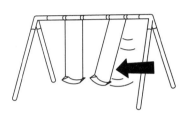

_ _ ing

_ ing

_ ing

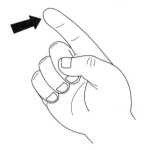

_ ing_ _

_ _inger

_ ing

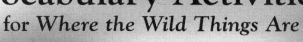

Vocabulary Activities
for *Where the Wild Things Are*

Pre-reading Activity: It is important that students understand the word *wild* before reading the story. Write the word *wild* on the board and tell students that Max gets in trouble for acting wild. Ask students what kinds of wild things Max might have done to get in trouble. Have students think of behaviors they have gotten in trouble for. List all responses web-style around the word *wild*. Ask students to explain the difference between a wild animal and a tame one (or a pet). Consider taking students outside to give them a few minutes to "act wild." Then, have students illustrate themselves acting wild. Have students copy the word *wild* on the tops of their papers. Encourage students to use their imaginations to add details to their drawings, and include writing from the class web. Display the illustrations on a bulletin board titled "Mr./Ms. ____'s Wild Things."

During-reading Activity: Help students learn vocabulary from the book while exposing them to the use of context clues. Prior to reading, display the following vocabulary words on index cards: *terrible, forest, mischief, rumpus*. Read each word and have students repeat it. Ask students if they can describe what each word means. Accept any responses, then tell students that sometimes it is easier to figure out what a word means when it is not "all by itself" but is in a sentence with clues from the other words or pictures. Tell students to look and listen for the words in the story as you read. Pause when you encounter one and guide students to define the word using context clues. For example, pause after reading the sentence " 'And now,' " cried Max, 'let the wild rumpus start!' " (*Where the Wild Things Are*, page 22). Ask students to guess what the word means again. Then, say, "Let's see what Max and 'wild things' have started doing on the next page." As you flip through the next few wordless pages, ask students, "What does it look like they are doing here?" Students will answer "Playing, having fun, going wild, etc." Ask, "So, do you think the word *rumpus* means something like having a party or playing? Would that make sense?" As you use this method, let students point out their own context clues for defining new words.

Post-reading Activity: This book is an excellent tool to teach the concepts of real and fantasy. After reading, make a chart with two columns labeled *Real* and *Fantasy*. Explain that the word *real* means it can really happen, while the word *fantasy* means it could never happen. Flip through the book's pages, reviewing the main events, and ask students to name things from the book that could be real. List these responses in the first column. Guide students as necessary. For example, ask, "What about Max wearing a wolf suit? Is that something that could happen in real life? Could a child in a costume be real?" Then, go back through the book and look for fantasy elements. (By going through the book twice, students are able to focus on only one element at a time, which will lessen confusion.) After completing the chart, have students complete copies of the Real or Fantasy? reproducible (page 153). Instruct each student to think of something real and something that is fantasy, such as boy/monster, and illustrate both things.

Real or Fantasy?

vocabulary reproducible for
Where the Wild Things Are

Name_____ Date _____

Think of something that is real and something that is fantasy. Draw a picture of your two ideas.

Real

Fantasy

Pre-reading Activity: Prior to reading the book, show students some of the text. Point out how some pages have many words, while others only have a few. Explain that the pictures tell most of the story. Also point out how some words are in all uppercase letters. Tell students that the author did this to help the reader read the book fluently—with expression and at just the right pace. Ask students how they think words in all uppercase letters should be read. Read some of these words with the students, and encourage them to put emphasis on words in all uppercase letters. Tell students to watch and listen for this when you read the book.

During-reading Activity: As you read aloud, pause after reading the pages about the forest growing. Ask students what is missing on the page that reads, "That very night in Max's room a forest grew" (*Where the Wild Things Are*, page 7). Say, "You see how there is no period here? For that reason I know that I have to keep my voice going to the next page, but I take a little breath so you can hear how the forest is growing and growing. See how the author put the words *and grew* by themselves on one page? That is why I chunk them together." Read the three pages that describe the forest growing again, so that students can hear the appropriate pauses and grouping of words. Then, have students echo read these three pages so they can "feel" how the words and the pauses "go with" the pages turning.

Post-reading Activity: Record yourself reading the book aloud with appropriate pauses for page turning. Set up a listening center where students can listen to the tape as they follow along in the text. This book's text format lends itself well to this activity because students can practice tracking print (pointing to the words) as they hear the tape. To encourage students to try to keep up and point to the text as they listen, have them make "terrible claws" like those of the wild things in the book. Give each student a copy of the Terrible Claws Pattern reproducible (page 155) to cut out. Help each student wrap the paper strap around her hand and tape it in place. Show her how to use the claws to point to each word as she reads and listen to the tape.

Terrible Claws Pattern
fluency reproducible for
Where the Wild Things Are

Name_____ Date _____

Cut out the claws. With your teacher's help, tape them around your hands. Use them to touch the words as you read.

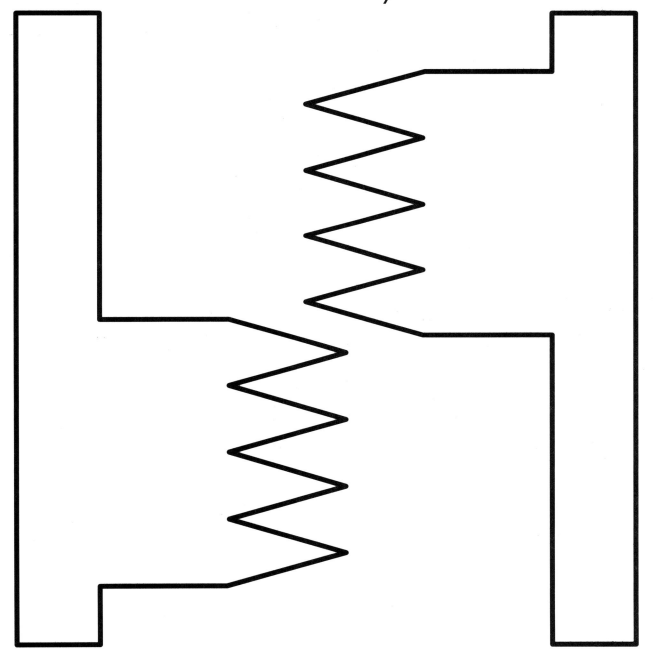

Pre-reading Activity: Tell students that a good reader previews a book before reading it. To do this, tell students that they should read the title, look at the cover, and take a "picture walk" through the book. Tell students that they can take "picture walks" by flipping through the pages and looking at the pictures to get clues about the story. Take a "picture walk" with students, pausing at each page to have students comment on what they see as well as what they think is happening on each page. Encourage students to see if some of their thoughts were accurate when you read the story.

During-reading Activity: Pause on the wordless pages after the "wild rumpus" starts (*Where the Wild Things Are,* page 22) and have students write text for these pages. Discuss what the text might say for each page. Have students dictate sentences to you. Write them on sentence strips and carefully attach them to the pages with paper clips (if you are using a big book version), or write them on small strips of paper if you are using a regular-sized book. Reread the book with the new text inserted.

Post-reading Activity: Give a copy of the Story Sequencing reproducible (page 157) to each student. Have students cut out the story strips. Read them aloud and have students glue them in the correct order on sheets of construction paper. To extend the activity, assign small groups to act out the sentences. After students put them in order, read each strip and let the corresponding group act out the scene silently.

Story Sequencing

comprehension reproducible for
Where the Wild Things Are

Student's Name _____   Date _____

Cut out the story strips below. Put them in the right story order and glue them to a piece of construction paper.

A forest grew in Max's room.

Max went home.

Max played with the wild things.

Max was acting wild.

Max got sent to bed.

Max met the wild things.

Max sailed away in a boat.

Answer Key for Activity Pages

This answer key includes information for pages that have definite answers. Also included are names of all pictures students are asked to identify. Answers are not included for games, drawing activities, activities in which students hold up cards during reading, storytelling activities, manipulative spelling activities, and other activities where individual and group participation are oral.

Brown Bear, Brown Bear, What Do You See? by Bill Martin, Jr.
page 9: Picture names are car, tree, cheese, sheep, fish, and mouse. Bears with tree, cheese, and sheep should be colored; bears with car, fish, and mouse should not be colored.
page 11: Pictures of bear, bird, bat, and boat should be colored blue; pictures of gate and cloud should not be colored.

Chicka Chicka Boom Boom by Bill Martin, Jr. and John Archambault
page 19: Picture names are fan, can, cat, tree, hat, and knee. Fan and can should have lines drawn to the an tree; tree and knee should have lines drawn to the ee tree; cat and hat should have lines drawn to the at tree.
page 21: Letters should be pasted in alphabetical order.

Corduroy by Don Freeman
page 29: Pictures names are zipper, mitten, giraffe, hammer, rabbit (or bunny), and balloon. Middle sounds are /p/, /t/, /r/, /m/, /b/ or /n/ (rabbit or bunny), and /l/. Students should write these letters in the middle sound blanks. Ending sounds are /r/, /n/, /f/, /r/, /t/ or /y/, and /n/. Students should write these letters in the ending sound blanks.
page 33: Store, unhappy, lost, napping, wanted, and friends should be circled.

Goodnight Moon by Margaret Wise Brown
page 41: The letter g should be written in each blank. The rock should be circled for gate, gorilla, goose, goat, and girl. The feather should be circled for gem, gingerbread, gerbil, and giraffe.
page 43: The picture should be colored according to directions.

Green Eggs and Ham by Dr. Seuss
page 49: Picture names are bee, coat, socks, jar, chain, and park.

If You Give a Moose a Muffin by Laura Joffe Numeroff
page 63: Students should match the muffin halves to make the following words: homemade, blackberry, grandmother, cardboard, something, and clothesline.
page 67: Answers will vary; students may list: the boy gives a moose a muffin; the moose asks for jam; the boy gives him jam; the moose eats the rest of the muffins; he asks the boy to make more; they prepare to go to the store; the moose asks for a sweater; he notices a missing button; he asks for a needle and thread; he sews the button back on; the moose asks for socks; he makes sock puppets; he asks for cardboard and paint to make scenery; he gets behind the couch; he asks for something to cover his antlers; the boy gets the moose a sheet; the moose tries it on and scares himself when shouting "Boo;" the moose cleans up the mess and washes the sheet; the moose starts to hang it out to dry; he sees the blackberry bushes; and finally he asks the boy for jam and a muffin to go with it.

In the Tall, Tall Grass by Denise Fleming
page 69: Students should sort these word and picture cards into piles: mop and stop, cap and map, and rug and bug.
page 71: Under the caterpillar, students should write the letters cr and m to make the words crunch and munch. Under the hummingbird, words should be dip and sip. Under the bee, words should be strum and hum. Under the bat, words should be loop and swoop. Under the rabbit, words should be hop and flop. Under the snake, words should be slide and glide.
page 73: Pictures names are hummingbird, bird, ant, snake, beetle, mole, frog, rabbit, and bat.

Leo the Late Bloomer by Robert Kraus

page 79: Shh-ing tiger should have could, wouldn't, and should under it. Shouting tiger should have late, bloomer, and Leo under it.

page 83: PIcture names are owl, crocodile, elephant, owl, plover, and snake.

Miss Bindergarten Gets Ready for Kindergarten by Joseph Slate

page 89: Picture names are apple, ball, cake, doll, egg, feather, goat, hat, igloo, jar, kite, leaf, mouse, net, octopus, pig, queen, ring, skunk, tree, umbrella, vase, window, X-ray, yo-yo, and zipper.

page 93: Picture names are ball, swing or swinging, brushing teeth, telephone, reading, eating. Swinging, brushing teeth, reading, and eating should be colored

The Napping House by Audrey Wood

page 99: Picture names are horn, necklace, net, hammer, nest, nail, hand, horse, hat, needle, heart, and house. Students should place horn, hammer, hand, horse, hat, heart, and house in one pile, and necklace, net, nail, and needle in another pile.

page 107: Pictures should be pasted together in the following order, from left to right and top to bottom: 1. Flea bites mouse; 2. Mouse startles cat; 3. Cat jumps on dog; 4. Dog jumps on boy; 5. Boy trips over grandmother;
6. Grandmother breaks bed

No, David! by David Shannon

page 109: Picture names are cake, sheep, boat, kite, wheel, comb, lion, music, nose, table, juice, cheese. The pictures should be sorted by long vowels. Long /a/ = cake, table. Long /e/ = sheep, wheel, cheese. Long /i/ = kite, lion. Long /o/ = boat, comb, nose. Long /u/ = music, juice.

page 111: The b should be written on the line to make the word boy. The g should be written on the line to make the word good. The e should written on the line to make the word bed. The t should be written on the line to make the word toys. The d should be written on the line to make the word bad. The a should be written on the line to make the word ball.

page 117: Students should draw as follows: Characters: The characters are David and his mother. Problem: David always gets into trouble and his mother tells him no and sends him to time out. Solution: David's mother tells him that yes, she does love him.

Silly Sally by Audrey Wood

page 119: First row: Picture names are spoon, ball, squirrel, and sock; ball should be marked with an x. Second row: Picture names are stove, swings, seesaw, and airplane, jet, or plane; airplane should be marked with an x. Third row: Picture names are sled, stroller, goose, and star; the goose should be should be marked with an x.

page 121: The p should be circled and written on the line to make pig. The d should be circled and written on the line to make dog. The c should be circled and written on the line to make cat. The j should be circled and written on the line to make jet. The c should be circled, the picture name is cup. The s should be circled, the picture name is sun.

There Was an Old Lady Who Swallowed a Fly by Simms Taback

page 129: Picture names are fly, spider, horse, cat, bird, dog, and cow. Invented spelling is acceptable for this activity.

page 131: The letter y should be written in each blank. Long /e/ should be circled for kitty and baby. Long /i/ should be circled for cry and frying pan.

page 133: Students should draw lines to match words and pictures.

Answer Key for Activity Pages

The Very Hungry Caterpillar by Eric Carle

page 139 The words *yo-yo, yes, yell,* and *yard* should be circled in yellow. The words *tiny, happy, grouchy,* and *busy* should be circled in green. The words *cry, why, my,* and *shy* should be circled in red. The sun should be colored yellow, the caterpillar should be colored green, and the butterfly should be colored red.

page 147 Picture names are egg, nice green leaf, moon, caterpillar, sun, apple, pears, plums, strawberries, oranges, chocolate cake, ice cream cone, pickle, Swiss cheese, salami, lollipop, cherry pie, sausage, cupcake, watermelon, caterpillar with a stomachache, cocoon, butterfly.

Where the Wild Things Are by Maurice Sendak

page 151 Picture names are <u>sw</u>ing, <u>k</u>ing, <u>r</u>ing, <u>f</u>inger, <u>st</u>inger, and <u>w</u>ing. Students should write sw, k, r, f, er, st, and w in the blanks.

page 157: The sentences are in the following order: 3, 7, 6, 1, 2, 5, 4. Students should arrange cards in the correct order.